"Reading Alisa Kasmir
conversation with a clo
restful walk alongside t
and Christian traditions, ...
unmentioned, like the Hindu, Buddhist, and Islamic. I highly recommend
this pleasant, musical, and personal read both to those working in
spiritual direction, as well as for spiritual practitioners looking to share
and mirror their own experiences."

> —Dr. Annewieke Vroom, expert in comparative philosophy and
> religious diversity, lecturer at Utrecht University, the Netherlands

"This profound book writes about what is at stake in the intimate
relationship and interaction of spiritual directors with those who yearn
for human flourishing in uncertain and difficult times, and who seek to
discern the ultimate orientation of their spiritual journey. The book calls
for the spiritual director to seek simply to be there and to be available
(*hineni*) for the other one in a perceptive, covenantal relationship . . . it
depicts this availability to the other as a challenge and even a risk, because
it requires complete connection, unconditional commitment to and
vulnerability before the other, sometimes at the cost of one's own needs
and knowledge—or even at being confronted with one's own helplessness
and incapacity for spiritual direction."

> —Pieter G.R. de Villiers, Professor of New Testament Studies
> University of the Free State, South Africa

"In Genesis 22, the fascinating and shocking story of Isaac's sacrifice, Abraham says *hineni* three times, 'here I am': the first time to God, the second time to his son, and the third time again to God. Alisa Kasmir names the willingness that these words express as the fundamental attitude of spiritual directors. By being open-minded and vulnerable, space is created for directors to perceive God's word in the narratives of their directees. Kasmir does not keep a monologue. Six seasoned spiritual directors affirm her argument with their own real-life experiences. Kasmir is expressive and succinct at the same time; she never loses sight of the common thread, *hineni*. Her story is inspiring and enchanting, pleasant for colleagues and for many others."

—Charles Caspers, Titus Brandsma Institute, Nijmegen

"*Hineni* is a way of seeing, of being, and of relating to the world. 'It means to say (in Hebrew) "Here I am for you, with you." ' Taking as point of departure the often puzzling, not to say shocking, midrash of Genesis 22 (Abraham's sacrifice of his son Isaac), and drawing on her rich religious background (Jewish, Christian, Carmelite, Benedictine), Kasmir weaves an inviting *lectio divina* to elucidate the art of spiritual direction. One will not read Genesis 22 in the same old way again. And one will view spiritual direction with a new sense of presence—to God, and to the companion on the way. The inclusion of eight personal interviews from an interreligious perspective show how *hineni* can be lived across interdenominational and interfaith lines."

—Helen Rolfson, OSF, Professor Emerita of Theology, Saint John's University School of Theology/Seminary, Collegeville, MN

"I have read many interpretations of Genesis 22—the story of Abraham's near-sacrifice of his son, Isaac. I probably suspected all that could be said had been. Then Kasmir comes at it from a fresh angle, like Emily Dickinson's 'tell all the truth, but tell it slant.' 'I will not tell you how you should or could or ought or must respond *hineni* to the one before you. Rather, I offer a mirror for your own approach,' she says. Reading Kasmir may be for you, as it is for me, not just looking in the mirror, but going through the looking glass to a new adventure."

—Patrick Henry, former executive director, Collegeville Institute for Ecumenical and Cultural Research

Hineni

In Imitation of Abraham

Alisa Kasmir

LITURGICAL PRESS

Collegeville, Minnesota

www.litpress.org

Cover design by Monica Bokinskie. Cover photo by Esa Kasmir.

William Stafford, excerpt from "Yes" from *The Way It Is: New and Selected Poems*. Copyright © 1994 by William Stafford. Reprinted with the permission of The Permissions Company, LLC on behalf of Graywolf Press, Minneapolis, Minnesota, graywolfpress.org.

2 3 4 5 6 7 8 9

Library of Congress Cataloging-in-Publication Data

Names: Kasmir, Alisa, author.
Title: Hineni : in imitation of Abraham / Alisa Kasmir.
Description: Collegeville, Minnesota : Liturgical Press, [2020] | Includes
  bibliographical references. | Summary: "A resource to anyone
  interested in spirituality beyond easy answers or (in)convenient labels
  and an exploration of what it truly means to be present—to yourself,
  to the one before you, and to the one we call God"—Provided by
  publisher.
Identifiers: LCCN 2019029637 (print) | LCCN 2019029638 (ebook) |
  ISBN 9780814688052 (paperback) | ISBN 9780814688304 (epub) |
  ISBN 9780814688304 (mobi) | ISBN 9780814688304 (pdf)
Subjects: LCSH: Abraham (Biblical patriarch)—In rabbinical literature.
  | Bible. Genesis, XXII, 1-19—Criticism, interpretation, etc. |
  Spirituality—Biblical teaching. | Spiritual life—Biblical teaching.
Classification: LCC BS1235.52 .K38 2020 (print) | LCC BS1235.52 (ebook)
  | DDC 222/.11092—dc23
LC record available at https://lccn.loc.gov/2019029637
LC ebook record available at https://lccn.loc.gov/2019029638

To Esa and Josha, my sons,
who challenge me every day to live *hineni*,
and to Becca and Pippa, my Labradors,
who show me how it's done.

Contents

Dear Reader,

Thank you for picking up this book. I hope that reading it will give you an idea of what it means to be present, in flesh and blood, to the mystery of another person, and about what it means to say, "Here I am for you, with you." *Hineni* is a way of seeing the world, of being in it and relating to it, and so, although this book applies theory specifically to the practice of spiritual direction, there is meaning to be found in these pages, whether you are involved in spiritual direction or not.

My first career was as a classical singer, a profession in which listening and being present are essential. The connection with spiritual direction was clear to me from the beginning. Both ask you to get out of the way and to let the music sing in you.

These days, I spend an unusual amount of time in the company of nuns. Kurt Hansen, a friend from Northwestern University, where we both studied music and sang in the chapel choir, sent a book one Christmas: Kathleen Norris's *The Cloister Walk*. It made me curious enough to fly in from the Netherlands for a visit. The Benedictine sisters in St. Joseph, Minnesota, live and model the kind of presence I write about. They call it "listening with the ear of the heart."

My dogs also act as living examples of *hineni*. The Netherlands is a great place to live if you love dogs. Dogs are welcome in most places—restaurants, stores, public transportation, schools—you get the idea. They can, in turn, be counted on to be well-behaved and socialized. It's a win-win situation.

It works well for me. My Labradors and I have been walking around town for over twenty years now. We have been stopped to talk so often on the streets of Kralingen, the part of Rotterdam where we live, that being stopped became hard to dismiss or ignore. Behind the narratives, people are telling us that they want to be seen. They want to matter. They want a friendly face to receive their stories. They are the real reason that first Becca, and now Pippa and I walk to the stores. Those who shared their concerns, pain, and questions were, I believe, showing me who I am, and calling me to spiritual direction.

In Imitation of Abraham, the subtitle, might make you wonder what is being imitated. Partly, it is an intended play on Thomas à Kempis's *De Imitatione Christi.* Just as he did not suggest that we become carbon copies of Jesus, but that we find the resonance, the universality in Jesus' example, and make it particular again in ourselves, imitating Abraham does not mean offering one of your children as a sacrifice. I offer a perspective on the Abraham and Isaac paradigm, as told in Genesis 22, based on the response, *"Hineni."* See what resonates in you, what of it you might make your own.

Ultimately, to say *hineni* is to learn something about your relationship with God and others, how you see God in the one before you, and about who you are in your core. Are you ready? As we used to say when singing through a particularly challenging score, I'll meet you at the double-bar line.

Warm greetings,
Alisa

Acknowledgments

Many people have lived *hineni* to me during the writing of this book. Without them, I would not have been able to do it. I thank them for being willing, open, and receptive in the moment (in some cases, an awful lot of moments) to this one before them.

To the women of Saint Benedict's and St. Scholastica's monasteries in Minnesota, where this work began and ended, whose examples strengthen me on my road, thank you. To all who read drafts and offered comments, thank you. To Sister Jonathan Herda, whose seeing me in the hall helped me to see differently, thank you. To Sister Kathryn Casper, who generously passed on papers, books, and decades of wisdom on spiritual direction, stirring my interest, thank you. To Sister Renée Domeier, for her keen editorial eye, thank you. To Sister Mara Faulkner, for challenging me to find the question I was afraid to ask and reminding me to sing with my own voice, thank you. To the scholars of Studium, for an enquiring and open atmosphere, and especially to Patrick Henry, for enthusiastic encouragement, guidance, and editorial input, thank you. To Sister Ann Marie Biermaier, head of Studium, for her generosity in providing space and giving sensitive feedback, thank you.

To the questionnaire respondents—Awraham Soetendorp, Leo de Jong, Blanche Bunting, Peter Korver, Jana Preble, and Hein Blommestijn—who unstintingly shared their wisdom, even though it took, in some cases, far more than two hours, thank you. To Leo, who helped me to see why I should keep going each time I was ready to quit, thank you. To Hein, who acted as academic and spiritual advisor to the final version of this book, thank you. And to Pippa, gorgeous Labrador, constant companion, and joyful, tail-wagging example of *hineni*, thank you—and extra treats!

To Carrie Gordon, friend since childhood, whose suggestions often freed the compassion from the rubble, thank you.

To Robert Cribb, professor of history at ANU in Canberra, and longtime friend, for casting his expert academic eye over various versions and keeping my artistic tendencies in check, thank you.

To Charlie Preble, Jana's husband, priest, carpenter, poet, and friend, who suggested and supported all along the way, thank you. And to Jana, who offered insights and helped ensure the questionnaire was clear and non-leading, thank you.

To Esa Kasmir, my firstborn, who photographed and designed the cover, and helped with all sorts of computer questions, thank you.

To Robin Lee, best friend, proofreader, cheerleader, unflappable receiver of grumbling and moaning who listened to every word I wrote, and chief ally on the road of life, thank you.

Introduction

More than Just Showing Up

The question at the heart of spiritual direction is how to meet the mystery of the other. *Hineni* is not an answer to the mystery. It is a response to the challenge, a response from the space where mystery and oneness meet. *Hineni*, "here I am," means much more than just showing up.[1]

My experience of spiritual work with people in both formal and informal settings affirms my intuition that, in the depth of their beings, people do not want advice or answers. They do not want to be repaired or fixed. They want to matter, to be seen. They want someone to witness their story, to bear with them, to bear it with them. A spiritual director listens for the story behind their story—God's story unfolding in them—and lifts it so that it can be seen and heard and made more visible to them.

This is true for homeless people and people living with dementia, as well as priests and poets and baronesses. It is true for people of faith and people who say they have none. Spiritual direction responds to the question, "*Ayekah*? Are you there for me?" by listening with the ear of the heart, like the Benedictines, by being open, willing, and receptive. By saying, "*Hineni*."

"There is no good English equivalent for the Hebrew '*hineni*,'" says *The Jewish Study Bible*. "The term indicates readiness, alertness, attentiveness, receptivity, and responsiveness to instruction."[2] The definition stresses readiness to respond rather than control. The verb "indicates" is directional. It is the "direction" of spiritual direction: *toward*. Spiritual directors serve as instruments or vessels, making space for the directee to become.

Hineni as a response, let alone a way of life, is an ideal. The ideal stands in tension with our lived reality, which is bound to fall short. It is just not possible to maintain presence to everyone and everything all the time. Still, we can catch glimpses of the ideal, in moments that tend to defy words, moments that reveal something undeniable in the now and pull us toward the horizon of that ideal.

Hineni happens—it is. It is a state of being in relation to things not yet known, so it cannot be set in stone. In a sense, we cannot be exploring what we are exploring. When something is written, it is nailed down. It is *this* and therefore not *that*. But what we are trying to speak about is in the cracks.[3] In an attempt to grasp something that is not apprehendable, we dissect and objectify. The very thing that is essential for relationship—separateness—also divides. It makes distinctions and definitions.[4] Grasping the reality of *hineni*—its mystery—from the inside is not possible.

And yet we have to agree upon what we are talking about. I have defined *hineni* as *an open, willing receptiveness in the moment to the mystery of the one before you, based on the fundamental oneness underneath all relationship. It is both awareness and embodiment of connection and commitment.*

The definition reveals complementary and sometimes paradoxical pairs: mystery and oneness, awareness and embodiment, connection and commitment (from covenant for humanity), open to receive, directional and in the moment (being and becoming). Holding, rather than resolving, the paradoxes central to *hineni* is crucial to the spiritual direction encounter.

Hineni begins with standing before the unknowable mystery of the other, acknowledging that, no matter how well you think you know a person, the one before you is a godly mystery. His or her otherness and the chasm that separates you make him or her a mystery, but also essential for relationship. In that in between space of holy reverence, the other invites you to look over his or her shoulder at what he or she sees. As spiritual directors, that is what we do: we help the other explore his or her path as we both look out toward his or her ultimate orientation.

The best we can do with the mystery of the other starts here, with going beyond our version of reality. What is then revealed is not the mystery itself, but that there is that mystery and it is beyond our grasp. Director and directee are looking for and at that which is beyond them both.

At the same time, *hineni* comes from, and acknowledges, a sense of connectedness beyond separation, a connectedness that Sister Jonathan Herda sensed when she strode into the hallway of St. Scholastica's Monastery, proclaiming, "The God in me wants to meet the God in you." It is the sense conveyed in this stanza from the poem "Islands" by Muriel Rukeyser: "O for God's sake / they are connected / underneath."[5]

We're Talking about Mysticism

Lawrence Kushner defines a mystic as "anyone who has the gnawing suspicion that the apparent discord, brokenness, contradictions, and discontinuities that assault us every day might conceal a hidden unity."[6] That sense is simply conveyed in this old Hassidic story:

> In the beginning there was only the Holy Darkness, the source of life. The world and everything in it came from the heart of this Holy Darkness as a great ray of light. And then there was an accident. And the vessel containing the light of the world broke. And fragments of that light fell

into all events and all things and all people, where they remain deeply hidden until this very day. We are all born with the capacity to find the hidden light in everything. It is our task to lift it up and make it visible once again.[7]

A spiritual director is trained in lifting the shard, so that the other might discover his or her hidden light.

The how of being there for the other is inherent to the moment of asking, as it was for the villagers of Le Chambon-sur-Lignon, France, who—despite raids, arrests, internment, threats, and even executions—hid Jews during World War II. Thousands of Jews—many of them children—were saved by this town.

When interviewed years later about the reasons for their actions, the villagers consistently did not understand the question. "Who else would have taken care of them if we did not? . . . We were doing what had to be done . . . what has that to do with goodness?"[8] For them, there was no why. There was only seeing what was before them, being moved, and responding.

Hineni cannot be made, or planned, any more than God can be controlled or summoned at our will. It is not an act of will, but an attitude of willingness. "Willingness implies a surrender of one's self-separateness, and entering into an immersion in the deepest processes of life itself. It is a realization that one already is a part of some ultimate cosmic process and it is a commitment to participation in that process."[9]

It's Personal—Singing as a Metaphor for *Hineni*

Hineni is, of course, personal. For me, it is an extension of my life as a singer.

A singer needs presence in order to function well in the job. The kind of presence needed for singing is a good metaphor for the spiritual direction relationship.

The singer needs to be present to the music and to fellow musicians. To be present to them all requires a very attentive sort of listening, in order for the music to be together and so that there is a balance of volume, colors, and sounds. This give-and-take relationship is, at its best moments, seamless: from many individual musicians, a transcendent oneness can emerge.

The audience is also part of the give and take. There are times when the music is flowing and people are somehow open to listening, and their listening adds something, too. The whole winds up being greater than the sum of the parts.

In order to sing, there must be space for resonance. A singer is basically a wind instrument. If you just blow between two vocal chords that vibrate, however, the result is unpleasant. The notes need to resonate in the spaces of the singer's body in order to have the color and the overtones that make sounds beautiful. If the spaces are filled in, the sound distorts.

To be present to the music means practice: scales and other vocal exercises so that the singer's voice is up to singing the music. In addition to practice, it helps to study—not just the notes, but the history and theory of music, which help the singer relate to a particular score. All of this work is important. It is part of honoring the musical gift that is present in the singer. But it is not the music.

Making music that touches the listener is more than a pretty voice and training. In a vulnerable paradox, the singer has to get out of the way and let the music sing in her. When the singer steps out onto the stage, she must forget technique, while using it at the same time. In order for there to be music, the singer has to be there. She has to sing. No singer, no music.

And yet, if there is too much self, if she gets in the way of letting the music sing through her, the performance winds up being forced or tedious. As the children's song "The Hokey Pokey" says, "You put your whole self in, you take your whole self out . . . that's what it's all about."

Mrs. R was in the day room, in a wheelchair, writhing in pain when I arrived one afternoon. It looked like she was having labor contractions. Her face was contorted. The nurses explained that she was barely conscious and unable to move. Would I sit with her? I pulled up a chair and took her hand. Was she holding my hand in return, or was what I felt part of the constant spasms racking her body? I don't know. It seemed she was in horrible, unimaginable pain and I felt helpless beside her. I stroked her cheek and her hair, and then something in me prompted me to sing: "Precious Lord, Take My Hand," "Deep River," "There Is a Balm in Gilead." The spasms seemed to lessen. I kept going for almost an hour, occasionally stopping to ask if she wanted more. Each time, her eyes locked with mine and urged me on. Slowly, her grip on my hand eased, and then her eyes seemed to say, "Enough." She relaxed a bit into her chair and closed her eyes. She died a few days later.

Singing all those years was training in being an instrument. It was training in being "a reed in the hand of God, to maintain a purposeful emptiness that receives the piper's breath and sings the song that is in his heart."[10] That is the core of singing. It is the core of spiritual direction. And it is the core of *hineni*.

What This Book Is Doing

In the chapters that follow, textual analysis of a paradigmatic Bible passage combines with stories and the lived experiences of a few seasoned veterans in the field, revealing the contemporary practical relevance to spiritual direction behind and beyond the larger-than-life but very real and full-of-life Abraham.

It has been said that the Bible is a book in which every story is about us. So I will examine Genesis 22 and see how it is about us, what in it resonates, what it tells us about what it is to be there for the other in relationship. The story shows that *hineni* is not always pretty and can, in fact, leave us feeling decidedly displaced.

Chapter 1 will focus on what it meant for Abraham to say *hineni*. *Lectio divina* with the text will yield Abraham's model through the paradoxical pairs. For the exploration of Genesis 22, a variety of commentaries and literary sources were consulted.

The focus on *hineni,* as a response to the mystery before us, means that the seminal works on Genesis 22 by Emmanuel Levinas and Søren Kierkegaard, while they provide valuable insights, are not central to my arguments.

Hineni can be, as Levinas suggests, a response in ethical responsibility to the face before us, a responsibility that presupposes a response, or ethics as the ultimate or universal. *Hineni can* be, as in Kierkegaard, the teleological suspension of ethics in the name of an absolute relationship. Both claim fundamental relationships, though the "with whom" differs. For purposes of this book, it is not important which relationship is fundamental, but, rather, *that* there is a fundamental relationship from which *hineni* is said. Neither "why" is, in the end, my point. What we are "imitating" is unique to the moment, and so, inimitable.

Chapter 2 looks at the implications of the Genesis story for spiritual direction. It responds to the questions, "What do Abraham's *hinenis* reveal to spiritual directors?" and "How do the paradoxical pairs as concepts apply to us?" These concepts are not meant to be left as theory, but to affect, or challenge, how we as spiritual directors interpret our practices.

The concepts led to the development of a questionnaire. The responses form the body of chapter 3. The meaning of *hineni* in the real-life experiences of the seasoned spiritual directors who responded is recounted in narrative. The collected wisdom will show eight unique ways of *hineni*, of making the Name, in imitation of Abraham.

Chapter 4 looks at both the particular—Abraham's and mine—and the universal implications of *hineni* for spiritual direction and for the journey of the reader, of all that has been discussed. I will not tell you how you should or could or ought or must respond *hineni* to the one before you. Rather, I offer a mirror for your own approach.

I

Genesis 22—A *Midrash*

Why This Story

The story of Abraham and Isaac has always disturbed me. I am in good company: Elie Wiesel, Kierkegaard and others have been bothered by it, too. Whoever delves into it eventually confronts a disturbing question: What kind of God asks you to kill your child to prove your love for him?

Disturbing: As a mother of sons, I note wryly that mothers tend to sacrifice *for* them. Why didn't God ask the mother to make the sacrifice? Why didn't Abraham consult his wife about the threat to their son? Unfortunately, disturbing questions are too often dismissed or avoided when interpreting this story, and that influences—I would

1

say distorts—both Christian and Jewish ideas about God. Some commentaries offered explanations; however, attempting to explain something that is inexplicable is not satisfying. It is going around the story instead of through it. Justifying Abraham's actions, or God's command, avoids entering the insanity of the story and our saying *hineni* to it.

Sermons typically exalt Abraham as the model of obedience. If we accept and attempt to emulate that model, we are following an example of someone willing to sacrifice his child—to have another pay the ultimate price for his beliefs—for his response to a demand from a God he does not understand. He understands neither the demand nor God.

Despite—or maybe because of—the fact that the story is so disturbing, this is the one that had to be tackled, gone through, in order to discover what it really means to say *hineni* to the one before me. You probably have difficulties with this story, too. I invite you to put them aside for the time being, as I have mine, as we enter into it.

Empty Spaces and Embodiment

The word *hineni*, as it is written in the Torah,[1] contains open spaces. There are no vowels written in the Torah. There are spaces or gaps between the consonants—the word reveals itself in its open spaces and the ambiguity allows us to discern multiple layers of meaning in the same written text.[2]

So we engage with the text, look at the spaces and ambiguities, and see.

In *On the Kabbalah and Its Symbolism*, Gershom Scholem tells a story of Rabbi Mendel of Rymanov and the mystical tradition that asks what was really heard in the receiving of the Ten Commandments. Scholem explores the Rabbi's idea and concludes that God did not communicate the commandments directly. God did not even communicate the first two, as some believe. All God gave was the first letter of the first word, "I" ("I am the Lord your God"), which in Hebrew is *aleph*.

It is often assumed that *aleph* is soundless. This is not quite true. Scholem notes that the sound of *aleph* is actually the click that your larynx makes in preparation to make a sound. It is the grounding for audible language, pregnant with all meaning, yet conveying none itself. Moses had to translate that nearly inaudible click. The mystical interpretation concludes that it becomes the job of each of us to give human, flesh and blood content to a sound.[3]

Each of us is an unspeakable word of God. Helping another to discover and live his or her content, is spiritual direction.

The Story

Abraham's history from the previous chapters of Genesis (11–21) gives us an idea of the relationship he had with Elohim (the Hebrew generic term for God; YHWH is the personal name of Israel's God) and how it was brought to the point of *hineni*.

Abraham, as a result of his first encounter with God, left his country, tribe and father's house. He had to "go forth"—*lech lecha*—in order to become.[4] Famine forces him into exile in Egypt. There, his wife Sarai is taken by Pharaoh.

Abraham battles the four kings. Then he has a child with the servant, Hagar, because Sarai still has not borne him the promised heir. He obeys God and circumcises himself and Hagar's son, Ishmael. As a part of this new covenant, Abram and Sarai are given new names by God: Abraham and Sarah.

Sarah is abducted once more before the promised son finally comes. Abraham sends Hagar and Ishmael away. Elohim consoles Abraham, assuring him that it is through Isaac that his descendants will be named.

In all of these encounters with Elohim, Abraham always did what was asked of him, even when it cost him dearly. Still, the response was never *hineni*.

That changes in chapter 22. "Abraham?" says the familiar voice. "*Hineni*—here I am," Abraham answers. "Take your son." Abraham, without a word, goes home. The next day, he packs up and leaves with his son, some servants and a donkey on a three-day journey.

When the destination is in sight, he leaves the servants and the donkey behind and proceeds with his son up the mountain. At the top, the two of them together build an altar for the sacrifice.

Isaac addresses his father and Abraham replies to him, "*Hineni b'ni*—here I am, my son." "What are we going to sacrifice?" "God will provide," the father responds, avoiding the whole truth. He then ties up his son, raises his knife, and is ready to strike, when a voice calls again, "Abraham, Abraham," twice. "Do not lay a hand on the boy." Isaac is released, a ram caught in a nearby thicket is sacrificed, and Abraham returns home.

The catalyst of the story—Elohim/YHWH—the one who instigates and drives the drama, appears as a voice, and through an angelic representative who calls from heaven. How we give content to these clicks, as Scholem would call them, is essential to understanding the core of what it means to say *hineni.* The voice fills in what is, ultimately, beyond words.

As previously noted, the word *hineni* itself has open spaces, and needs to be given human content. There are also spaces in the text which ask for the same.

There is a space between verses 2 and 3, which makes us wonder what went on in Abraham's mind and heart in the time between what he heard and when he awoke the next morning to prepare.

There is another similar space between verses 3 and 4: the three days, which Kierkegaard tells us last longer than the time separating us from the original event.[5] These spaces give room to imagine the agony Abraham must have felt at the horror of the sacrifice demanded of him.

Twice, in verses 6 and 8, father and son walk on together. That space is also not filled in. Many *midrashim* posit that, by the second time they walk on together, Isaac must have known what was going to happen, and Abraham knew that he knew. Still, they went.

Space (handwritten annotation in margin)

In the space between verses 12 and 13, Abraham notices the ram. When there is space, we notice things.

There is one more space, between verses 18 and 19. Abraham returns to his servants. But what about Isaac? Wiesel and others suggest that Abraham returns home without his son. We do not hear from Isaac again until chapter 24, and by then many years have passed.

All These Things

Before we launch into the text, I would like to share with you the relationship I bring to it, hoping it will invite you to do the same.

My relationship with the Bible developed at university. The house I grew up in had no Bible. We were culturally Jewish, but any sense of religion died with my paternal grandfather.

Grandpa Morty was an observant Jew, who went to *Shul* on Saturdays, something I think he looked forward to. He would often take me along, carrying me on his shoulders, despite the rule of not carrying anything on the Sabbath. When his friends would tease him about it, his smile would just get bigger, his blue eyes twinkling. That memory is written on my heart.

My Jewish roots do play a role in how I view the function of stories. I grew up in a household in which stories were not meant to convey facts, but a message. It was often said about my maternal grandmother that it took more than facts to convince her of something, which was true in more ways than one. And Grandma Freda was a grand storyteller.

So, for me, Biblical texts are not about communicating events with factual accuracy, nor is the Bible meant to prove or disprove a position. The stories convey larger truths; they keep revealing. They grow on you and you grow with them.

Kierkegaard has said that the Bible is a book in which every line is about you.[6] That makes it a book of discovery, too—a book meant to push the boundaries of reality. Such a book is meant to show that, in the very ordinary slog of life, the extraordinary hides in plain sight.

So that is my relationship with the Bible.

The one before me is another story. This Bible was given by my grade school music teacher for my eighteenth birthday. It is the first one I ever held in my hands. The inscription on the inside front cover reads: "May the words and knowledge contained herein bring as much beauty and inspiration into your life as your friendship and gift of singing have brought into mine." This nice Jewish girl is now (also) a practicing Christian who has studied spiritual direction with Carmelites and for whom a Benedictine monastery is a second home, so I guess it has.

It was this Bible that I was reading in my dorm room at Northwestern University, when something inside me urged me to say "yes"—to what, I had no idea. I still don't.

So, now that you have a sense of where the rest is coming from, and perhaps have had a chance to think about your own relationship as well, let's open the book and start to read.

The Text[7]

Genesis 22:1

After these things Elohim tested Abraham. He said to him, "Abraham!" And he said, "Here I am."

Just as each of us brings a back story to the reading of a text, Abraham brings "these things," all of what has transpired between himself and Elohim with him, in him, to this moment. From all that has gone on previously within that relationship, Abraham can now say "*hineni*" for the first time. His connection has engendered a new sort of commitment, the import of which he does not (yet) fully understand. All that had come before pointed the direction for his inner compass. *Hineni*, when used in the Torah, indicates a turning point, a point of transformation. In this case, it seems that the transformation[8] is from an I-It relationship into an I-Thou one.

A very brief summary of Martin Buber's distinction between the two tells us that the participant/subject of an I-It relationship experiences the object of the relationship as a collection of qualities and quantities. The "I" is an observer more than an active participant. An I-It relationship can transform into an I-Thou relationship, through relationship with the object and then participating in something with that object. As a result, both are transformed by the relationship between them. Although most human relationships swing between the two, two subjects—an I and a Thou, not an I and an It—are essential for a covenantal relationship.[9]

From this relationship, this connection, comes the commitment of "just because." Elohim asks, "Abraham?" *Ayekah*? (Are you there for me?) Opening to encounter is inherently vulnerable, exactly because the question is not conditional: "If you love me, you will . . . ." There is no "if."

My sons reveal to me that I am their mother. When one of them calls himself my son, he acknowledges my motherhood. In turn, acknowledging my motherhood reveals to him that he is a son. So the created reveals to the Creator that he is the Creator. In turn, acknowledging the Creator reveals to the created that he is the created. To say *hineni*—here I am for you—is to (finally) acknowledge this mutually revealing, fundamental relationship, which is the foundation of "I am your God and you are my people."

The voice that Abraham hears, Scholem's "click," is familiar to Abraham. It is the voice that he has trusted, the one that has guided him throughout his long life. *Abraham? Ayekah? Where are you? Are you ready?*

Hineni, says Levinas, is the condition of readiness, of orientation, that precedes the question. It is knowing that you are your brother's keeper before the question is asked. The other *is* your business and, in fact, bestows you with identity.[10] This first *hineni* resonates with the sense of "I am because you are."

Genesis 22:2

He said, "Take your son, your only son Isaac, whom you love, and go to the land of Moriah, and offer him there as a burnt offering on one of the mountains that I shall show you."

Now Abraham hears what he has said "*hineni*" to. The instructions are in the imperative: take, go, offer.[11] Various *midrashim* note that Abraham did not argue, but perhaps should have argued. Some fill in an argument.[12] The command is so uncompromising and clear, and so personal, that argument within the relationship, in the moment, would seem to have been impossible. Most of us tend to think of arguments much later on, in retrospect. It is my sense that Abraham did not fill in this space, but rather received what he heard in stunned silence.

Genesis 22:3

Abraham rose early in the morning, saddled his donkey, and took two of his young men with him, and his son Isaac; he cut the wood for the burnt offering, and set out and went to the place in the distance that Elohim had shown him.

The words describing Abraham's actions imitate those of Elohim's request: he rose, saddled, took, split, and went.[13] Abraham does not speak. In the moment, he does what needs to be done.

Genesis 22:4-5

On the third day Abraham looked up and saw the place far away. Then Abraham said to his young men, "Stay here with the donkey; the boy and I will go over there; we will worship, and then we will come back to you."

Once again, the verbs imitate verse 2: you stay; we will go, worship, and come back.[14]

Three days pass, with Abraham walking with his secret. After three days—three days about which we have no information—the party arrives within sight of the goal. Imagine Abraham's grim determination. He is the only one who knows what they are setting out to do. From the time that they left, until the mountain is in sight, there is no recorded exchange. They walk in silence.[15] They did not fill in the space between them, but allowed it to be, to speak for itself.

Genesis 22:6-8

Abraham took the wood of the burnt offering and laid it on his son Isaac, and he himself carried the fire and the knife. So the two of them walked on together. Isaac said to his father Abraham, "Father!" And he said, "Here I am, my son." He said, "The fire and the wood are here, but where is the lamb for a burnt offering?" Abraham said, "Elohim himself will provide the lamb for a burnt offering, my son." So the two of them walked on together.

Now father and son have their only conversation of the entire episode.[16] Some commentaries note that Isaac calls out not just "father," but "*my* father." Where are you? Are you here for me? Abraham responds, "*Hineni b'ni*"—"Here I am, my son. I am here for you."

The exchange between father and son is tender. It is also an indication of an I-It relationship. Abraham seems to see his son (also) as necessary to the fulfillment of God's promise. Isaac is, on some level, an object, part of a transaction.

Furthermore, in Abraham's not quite telling what is going on, he is not only keeping Isaac from the truth about what they are doing, but also keeping his son from the truth about the father. It seems that Abraham may be upholding a false image of himself. Although Abraham has said *hineni* both to God and to Isaac, he still seems to be holding on to some illusions in both relationships.

Abraham now starts to be torn apart as he is confronted by the two conflicting, contradicting *hineni* responses. It seems that both relationships are fundamental, yet to say yes to one seems to necessarily exclude the other. This is the paradoxical reality of *hineni:* presence necessitates absence.

The text begins to reveal what it is to be bound in intimate relationship and unconditional love. We now start to feel what it costs Abraham to be receptive both to God and to his own son.

Father and son are bound to each other. Maybe it is exactly that binding that must be loosed, because of the *my*. We do not own each other—we do not *have* anything,[17] no matter how much we love or care. So much of parenting is having plans, ideas, and dreams dismantled. The parent has to make space for the child to be him- or herself.[18] Maybe *my* has become an obstacle to the process.

Being a parent means that you succeed if you have made yourself redundant, letting go of what, in a way, was never yours to begin with. Each child must individuate, be cut loose, in order to grow.

Abraham, too, must be cut loose—from his image of God, even from his need of God, for need tends to make an object of the other. The room to grow spiritually is what the Jewish mystics call *tzimtzum*: God making space for us to be ourselves.[19]

Genesis 22:9-11

When they came to the place that Elohim had shown him, Abraham built an altar there and laid the wood in order. He bound his son Isaac, and laid him on the altar, on top of the wood. Then Abraham reached out his hand and took the knife to kill his son. But the angel of YHWH/Elohim called to him from heaven, and said, "Abraham, Abraham!" And he said, "Here I am."

We now come to the climax of the drama. Once again, the verbs imitate—built, bound, laid, slaughter—a disturbingly deliberate sequence. The verbs convey a real sense of acting without stopping to weigh consequences.

This is the moment that Rembrandt captures so well—not once, but twice. *The Sacrifice of Isaac*, a painting from 1635, captures the moment of interruption, where understanding of reality until that moment is cut into by the intrusion of something else.[20] Abraham, knife in mid-air, is ready to strike, when the angel's voice calls. The angel grabs the father's right arm. The knife is suspended in midair.[21]

Rembrandt has depicted the exact moment when Abraham cries out "*hineni.*" There is anguish in his face, but also emptiness. Isaac's body is tensed. His face is covered by Abraham's hand. It seems the father cannot bear to have the son see what is happening.[22] Abraham's gaze is fixed on the angel.

The depicted moment is a moment of change in the text as well. Just as Abram ("mighty father") became Abraham ("father of many nations"), now God in relation to Abraham undergoes a change as well, from Elohim, meaning "The One(s)" or "containing all," to YHWH—I AM (here for you). It is a moment of profound awareness for Abraham, a new seeing, which translates immediately into the embodied (re)action of dropping the knife.

The second Rembrandt depiction, *The Sacrifice of Abraham*, an etching he made twenty years later, is less filled in and defined. The angel's body enfolds the father and each of the arms grasps one of Abraham's. Abraham's left arm holds the knife, while his right hand shields Isaac's eyes, rather than covering his whole face. He is seated in such a way that Isaac can kneel with his head on his father's lap.

Isaac's hands are not bound, but rather disappear under Abraham's robe. Abraham looks old and worn. His eyes are hollow—somewhere between desperate and vacant. The angel looks deep into Abraham's face with concern.[23]

Rembrandt is showing us, in that broken face, what it has cost Abraham to say *hineni* both to God and to his son[24]—the unspeakable cost of presence. Abraham *cannot*—that is, he has reached the end of his ability to argue and reason and think and even to be led by his feelings. He can't. This third *hineni* is uttered from the impossibility of the moment. He cannot be *hineni* for his son and go on with what he is about to do. Something has to break. Something does.

At this moment in the drama, Abraham seems to be sacrificing his future, and with it, the very covenant on which his faith is based.[25] It cannot be kept if there is no Isaac to keep it. This seems to confirm that there was a way in which Isaac was an It, an object to his father, a means.

Letting go of the knife is symbolic of Abraham's letting go of his idea of God. The transformation is so fundamental to his being that it changes his relationship with God, with others and with himself. The third *hineni* reveals a new divine name: "Here I am for you."

This is a first step in something new, as well as another step on the way. From here on, "Here I am" needs to become flesh. It accompanies a realization that God is not any longer, for Abraham, an externally occurring superpower, but one who moves him to becoming.

What is a covenant with the divine if one cannot live it on earth? It seems that Abraham was so engrossed, perhaps obsessed, by his "mission" that he could not see the person before him. Perhaps this is why the angel calls twice. Abraham has had to learn that the relationship with the divine is not only in ideas or theory, but in the flesh, in the face of the one before him. Perhaps the call was to "two" Abrahams: Abraham, the father, and Abraham, the dutiful servant.[26] Somehow, the either/or needed to become both/and.

Still, Abraham is at a point of nothingness. There was no retrospect in that moment to assure him that what he was doing would eventually turn out all right. Just the horrific feeling that sometimes accompanies doing what one's inner compass tells one to do.

A neighbor in Rotterdam told the following story. She was the mother of four small boys during the war, just trying to get through it, like everyone else. Then one night, a knock at the door. Unexpected and unsolicited. Would she be willing to take in a Jewish couple? She had never planned to hide anyone. Doing so risked not only her life, but the lives of her boys. She said she did not think about it, there was no time to think about it, and if she had stopped to consider the ramifications, she might have done differently.

She said yes. Her yes horrified her, even as she said it, but that was what she knew she had to do in that moment. In the middle of war, when so little was secure or certain, something inside told her. She made the decision, without assurance, knowing that she risked not only her life, but her boys' lives as well.

Genesis 22:12-18

He said, "Do not lay your hand on the boy or do anything to him; for now I know that you fear Elohim, since you have not withheld your son, your only son, from me." And Abraham looked up and saw a ram, caught in a thicket by its horns. Abraham went and took the ram and offered it up as a burnt offering instead of his son. So Abraham called that place "YHWH will provide"; as it is said to this day, "On the mount of YHWH it shall be provided." The angel of YHWH called to Abraham a second time from heaven, and said, "By myself I have sworn, says YHWH: Because you have done this, and have not withheld your son, your only son, I will indeed bless you, and I will make your offspring as numerous as the stars of heaven and as the sand that is on the seashore. And your offspring shall possess the gate of their enemies, and by your offspring shall all the nations of the earth gain blessing for themselves, because you have obeyed my voice."

We now move to the resolution of the drama. The reasoning of Elohim, "Since you have not withheld your son," forces us to confront another question, one, as Wiesel notes, of ethical suspension: Can inhumanity ever be a way for a person to move closer to God?[27] Behind Wiesel's questioning of Kierkegaard's "explanation" is the very human question, "Why?"

My God, my God, why hast thou forsaken me? This is the cry of the psalmist, and of Jesus on the cross. We can imagine that it was somewhere deep inside of Abraham, too. *Lama*—from *le ma*—does not ask for a reason, but a purpose.[28] *Hineni* implies that, whatever action is undertaken from that space is "just because"—in the moment and not for a reason. I would qualify that: without a reason, but not without a purpose or direction.

"Now I know." Walter Brueggemann comments:

> It is not a game with God. God genuinely does not know. And that is settled in verse 12, "Now I know." There is real development in the plot. The flow of the narrative accomplishes something in the awareness of God. He did not know. Now he knows. The narrative will not be understood if it is taken as a flat event of "testing." It can only be understood if it is seen to be a genuine movement in the history between Yahweh and Abraham.[29]

I am not sure we can know anything about God, or that God has beingness or can know. But what Brueggemann's emphasis does imply is now-ness. Lawrence Kushner posits that "there is no such thing as time for God. God experiences the past, the present, and the future as one present continuous reality. And so that means that for us the world's coming into being is continuous. And we come close to God when we are willing to experience the world in the same way."[30]

The word "since" implies that the blessing was conditional. I think that the condition of receiving a blessing is the attitude of willingness: to receive a blessing, one must be receptive, open, willing. In other words, one must say "*hineni.*" The willingness may also be a tacit acknowledgment that "your son, your only son" is not Abraham's, but ultimately God's. We do not own our children, however much we love them.[31]

A covenant is different from a contract. The latter is usually financial and legal and stipulates promises, responsibilities, and privileges. It is essentially an exchange of goods and services. A covenant is, essentially, *establishing a relationship*, a binding between people or between people and God. It is not an exchange of goods and services, but of selfhood. "I am yours and you are mine."[32]

As long as Abraham clings to Isaac as an object, as the only way to keep the covenant, the relationship has a transactional quality. He uses the relationship with his son as a means of seeking a security that precludes trust. The covenant behind the covenant tells us that trusting God means "we do not make our own fruitfulness. As children of God, all live from the creative force of love."[33]

Hineni reveals a terrible side of unconditional love: it cannot abide walls or control. *Lech lecha* inevitably means letting go of the objects of our love. Letting go of the other for the sake of the other, letting go of God for the sake of God, though counterintuitive, is the only option. It is painful, in love, to know that love ultimately must be sacrificed for its own sake.

Participating in this experience has transformed both parties and the relationship. Abraham has now *become* and is ready to commit to the covenant as a subject. This third *hineni* indicates his open willingness for that transformation. Abraham's way of seeing Elohim is transformed, and so is his way of seeing himself.[34]

In Genesis 17, Abram is called to become who he is meant to be: Abraham, father of many nations. In Genesis 22, Elohim has become I AM. We do not know who, what, or where God was before he was God. He is God only in relationship to his creation.[35] And we are, because God is. Each derives "being" from the other, and the relationship is their being. In it, both are bound and free.

Genesis 22:19

So Abraham returned to his young men, and they arose and went together to Beer-sheba; and Abraham lived at Beer-sheba.

Abraham picks up and goes home, *vayashav—he* returned.[36] Some commentaries say without Isaac. I agree. He has sacrificed his son, all right, or, at least, who he thought his son was to him. Wiesel points out that their relationship surely bore the wounds of what transpired on that mountain. Abraham has sacrificed a flesh-and-blood relationship, comfort, and security for that ultimate horizon that he keeps walking toward and never reaches. How comforting is that covenantal relationship as he walks home? When he tells his wife? I can imagine that Abraham does not feel justified, but empty.

This is Abraham's last recorded encounter with God.[37] Abraham's letting go of what he thought was his, is truly about *having* nothing. Not even the constant reassurance of a relationship with God. Perhaps trusting the relationship has come to mean even letting go of needing or wanting reassurance. The *I* has come to know the self because of the *Thou*. Now "I can go on alone," knowing "I have heard and seen."[38] Abraham has heard and seen.

Abraham now has to make the name—here I am for you—himself. By making the Name, God *is* there. Maybe Abraham does not need voices anymore. *Hineni* has become a space from which to act and be moved, without having to have a reason.

Chapter Conclusions

Being and Becoming

How to meet the mystery of the other? In this case, how does Abraham meet the mystery of a God who, having given him a son, would take that son away? How do we begin to have a relationship with the One who *is* not, who is unknowable?

Genesis 22 says that the "how" has to do with becoming who we are. *Hineni* is a world in a word. It is not until chapter 22 that the word *hineni* is uttered. It took a while for the relationship to move from the transactional sense of "I am your God and you are my people" to the transformational.

To have that sort of relationship, Abraham had to become who he was.

Becoming is directional. Becoming is the journey. This is what each encounter with the divine was moving him toward—go out in order to become. He had to let go of whatever was holding him back. An agonizing, all-encompassing experience may be the only thing strong enough to bring an unadorned confrontation, break images,[39] and bring us face to face.

Abraham needed to come face to face with the *lama*, the purpose for which he had been living. To have a sense of purpose was to reposition from object of fate to subject of destiny, who can then have a subject to subject relation with the subject of his life. That is the covenant. The transition cannot be made without the willing consent of *hineni*.[40]

The new normal is that there is no more normal, no more taken-for-granted comfort or security. Abraham has been so deeply broken that broken is his new normal. Letting go of the security he thought he had "marks Abraham's life. Again and again, he had to renounce the desire for security and self-preservation, and, in the space of not knowing, become (increasingly) open for a God who will not be conformed to the framework of human logic."[41]

Abraham kept hearing "Go forth." What he encountered gradually showed him himself: "Go for yourself." Go, so that you can become.[42] Abraham needed to become his own holy place, truly himself, to have a covenantal relationship with God, and perhaps with his son. It is a journey to a holy land, indeed.

Embodiment

What we have just done is to give human content to the almost inaudible sound. The relationship of *hineni* is not "yes" when I feel like it, when it is convenient, or when it serves my ends. It is not a plan. It is "yes" in the moment. Yes, for Abraham, even though the cost was almost unbearable.

We suppose that when the shock wears off, Abraham would seek some comfort and assurance in the relationship for which he was willing to sacrifice all. But he does not get that. He does not hear from God again, as far as we know. The relationship between Abraham and God seems to move from a sense of security—a covenant and a son—through loss of both, into a space where no assurance is given or needed. The click has been filled with human content.

What would happen if you were to become who you are at your core? Then nothing outside is necessary anymore. There is no more "trying to be." You *are* I AM. Maybe Abraham did not need that voice anymore, because he had become *hineni.*

The problem with ideals is that even they can become prisons. Perhaps this is one of the shadows of *hineni.* At this beginning, middle, and end for Abraham, perhaps he is given his freedom by God the Father in the only way possible. Perhaps *tzimtzum,* space given in love, inevitably means cutting the ties that bind. Perhaps it means letting go of images of who we think God is, the God of our desire, so that God, too, can have the space to be ever more who or what God is, also in us. Perhaps God the Father lets go, so that Abraham can be himself.

Relationship, Connection, and Oneness

In the story, Abraham's relationships are ones in which trust has been built up over time. His responses come from that long-term relationship. But what about when the one before you is a stranger? This question, and the echo in Abraham's experience, point toward a oneness beyond mystery.

The echo in Abraham's experience can be found in Genesis 18, when he saw Elohim in the strangers at Mamre and welcomed them into his home as honored guests. Abraham, like Sister Jonathan, seems to have been honoring the God in the others, the God with whom he already has a relationship, so the strangers were strangers, and yet not.

And yet. Mary Magdalene thought she saw a gardener, until she recognized in him the face of one she knew. Something similar happened to the two disciples on the road to Emmaus. When I gave birth to each of my boys, they were handed to me by the doctor, who presented each one, saying, "Here is your son." Now, rationally, each one was a total stranger. We had never met. I knew nothing about them and they knew nothing about me. Yet we were also obviously bound, and, until the moment the cord binding us was cut, one. *Hineni* resonates with the memory of something within each of us that connects and even binds us.

Ultimate Mystery

"After all these things," this story still disturbs me. It should. Once we let go of the question "What kind of God would ask you to kill your own son?" and are done being indignant, something even more disturbing emerges.

The command seems to reveal something, if not about God, who is unknowable, then at least about our images of God. Brueggemann says that Genesis 22 tells us that "faith is a serious game. The call to Abraham is a call to live in the presence of this God who moves both toward us and apart from us . . . God is not 'reasonable.' God is not a logical premise who must perform in rational consistency."[43]

The command tells us that we have no idea who or what we are dealing with. *Mysterium tremendum et fascinans*. William Stafford expresses the sense of it in his poem "Yes":

> It could happen any time, tornado,
> earthquake, Armageddon. It could happen.
> Or sunshine, love, salvation.
>
> It could, you know. That's why we wake
> and look out—no guarantees
> in this life.[44]

II

Hineni: Making the Name and the Practice of Spiritual Direction

Abraham's story is not meant as a literal recounting of one man's life four millennia ago. The story is a myth: a grand narrative that expresses common human experience. Myth is not false; rather, it encapsulates truth about subjects that cannot be perceived fully through reason alone.[1]

What does *hineni* mean for us today, especially (but not exclusively) within the spiritual direction relationship?

The Business of the Words

William Stafford's poem is, in one way, as disturbing as is Genesis 22. His extreme images of the utter lack of control and unpredictability of that which shapes us lead me to a confrontational question regarding spiritual direction, the one I am afraid to ask, "What have I started here?"

Brueggemann says the question about "What kind of God?" must "not be explained, for it will not be explained." If we forgo explanation, we are led to the reality that God is God. Can we be prepared to meet such a radical God? Brueggemann notes that there are times when it is seductively attractive to find an easier, less demanding alternative to God.[2] We are warned.

And yet, spiritual direction is about seeking the business of the words, God's story in the other. That would seem to preclude the easier way. It would be "yes" to the way that leads through possible Armageddon or sunshine, toward becoming and in being, where we are set free. One thing is clear—we have no idea what we have said yes to.

We Have No Idea What We Have Said "Yes" To

In order to give a sense of what that can mean, I offer the following example, compiled from years of spiritual direction correspondence generously made available to me.

Sister M. has been a Carmelite for seventy-one of her ninety-four years. To describe her journey as humble, authentic, is an understatement.

Monastics sometimes refer to themselves as professional seekers of God. For Sister M., seeking with all her heart, which is the "yes," has become a severe grace.

In a way, her journey has imitated Abraham's. From a life that once seemed led by experiences of God working in her, and a deep assurance of God's love for her, she lives now, as she has lived for over thirty-five years, with the sense that God is essentially absent from her life. Her lived reality does not feel like *hineni*. It feels like God does not see her at all. What in Abraham has been retrospectively interpreted here as *tzimtzum*, feels to Sister M. like rejection, failure and abandonment, engendering fear and doubt.

How do you have a relationship with your heart's desire, when old, comforting images and illusions of God have fallen away and there is nothing to replace them, while at the same time it becomes clear that nothing but your heart's desire will satisfy?

The problem, as Sister M. notes, is that you cannot have God. God is "No Thing," and you cannot possess what is not. If even the child you bore is not yours to have, how can God possibly be? Slowly, the realization grows that what you have said "yes" to, what you have devoted your whole life to and that which is the desire of your heart, you cannot ever "have." So it seems that Sister M. is living a fundamental, perhaps *the* fundamental paradox at the heart of the spiritual life.

She has tried to make sense of it, but God does not make sense, so seeking purpose in suffering no longer comforts. Seeking solace within the familiarity of religious terminology no longer consoles. There is not much to cling to. And then surrender (which always takes place after a struggle when holding on no longer works), in which there is theoretically "more" God in you, feels to her like there is less. The more she seems to surrender, the worse she feels, because she sees there is ever more to surrender. She describes feeling powerless, being powerless to love and be loved.

Sister M. clearly recalls her moment of "yes": "The crucified Christ became alive to me, though I did not see him with my eyes. He asked me if I wanted to be transformed. He gave the answer: 'yes,' while I said a wordless 'yes' with my whole being. Sometimes I dare hope that my current situation has something to do with that promise way back in 1948, a promise I have never been able to forget."

Even though the image of Jesus crucified could have been a hint of what was to come, the full reality of the journey cannot be imagined at its onset. Who would ever say "yes," knowing that "yes" leads to the cross?

And yet. Something Bob Gay, an opera professor at Northwestern University for a quarter of a century, used to say to young singers seems to address this question: "If I had told you that following your heart would be this hard, you wouldn't have believed me."

"What I miss," Sister M. writes, "is not so much the inability to experience God, but the inability even to experience my own increasing surrendering into ever more nothing so that perhaps I could be of service to what God wishes to do in me. There is more, but words fail me. (Yet) in the depth of my depth, God is."

It is not that there is no hope or joy in Sister M.'s life, or that her whole life is darkness. She still knows what she calls "happiness in God." It is just not the only truth.

You might think that being in community would provide understanding and consolation for Sister M. But hers is a reality no one around her knows from the inside, and so it is a lonely place to be. Maybe it's a bit like living in the stripped-down reality of dementia. Those outside of your reality have no point of reference for what it is, yet at the same time they fear it and keep it at a distance so they can go about their ordinary religious lives. Maybe it's the monastic equivalent of a parent losing a child.

Her reality does not prevent her from noting with admiration when others are being loving and kind and helpful. It's just that she also sees that there is much busyness with and satisfaction in things that, from her perspective, are not the heart's true desire, and so are "nothing."

Prayer—in the sense of turning to God, which necessitates seeing the self as separate from God in order to be able to turn to God—is hard. When she is taken up in the silence where all is one, and she "is" no longer, then all is prayer. And yet, she is part of a monastic community, where prayers are central.

"God is too big," and yet the word "God" doesn't mean anything anymore. Sister M. wonders if any of what she was taught to believe in is true. She often feels herself without ground under her feet. "Former ways of having been 'destroyed' were child's play. My current situation, which leads nowhere, only gets worse. That is how I experience it. It is hopeless." Longing has long ago been replaced by emptiness. Love? She is not sure what that is anymore.

And yet, Sister M. does not give up. Perhaps because she says she has nothing to look forward to and questions the truth or value of what she looks back on, "yes," in the moment, to the moment, might literally be all there is. And so, each evening, before going to sleep, conscious of a fundamental inadequacy in God's overwhelming presence, she ends her day with the words, "Here I am." *Hineni*.

"It could, you know. No guarantees in this life."[3]

Awareness and Embodiment

Saying *hineni* to the one before me is, at first, a response to an interruption. To hearing the click. *Ayekah*, where are you, breaks into my understanding of reality by the intrusion of someone else.[4] Henri Nouwen once observed, "My whole life I have complained that my work was constantly interrupted, until I discovered that my interruptions were my work."[5]

As previously noted, the one before me, interrupting by his or her call, *ayekah*, calls me into being in relationship.

Responding *hineni*, here I am for you, affirms the humanity of the other. *Hineni*, awareness that the interruptions are my work, is awareness of the connection beyond the mystery of otherness through willingness to participate in the moment with him, by willingly putting aside my own interests in the moment of interruption. I have gone beyond myself to make space for others.

Awareness allows the space for us to *become the body*: the eyes, or hands or feet with which God looks compassion on the world.[6] When we say *hineni*, it is as if God is responding to the world through us.[7] Each time we lift up the broken shard of another, we are engaging in *tikkun olam*—"healing the world."[8] This is what is meant by "from a covenantal I-Thou relationship, for humanity."

It is what is behind Sister Jonathan's words. The God in me is that depth from which I can really see, and from there, act. It is what we see in Jesus each time he is moved to his depths with compassion, and from there, he acts—from the space where he and the Father are one.

Open to Receive

For the one before us, "all these things" got him or her to where they are now, in front of us. For us, "things" can get in the way of resonance. Think of Etty Hillesum clearing rubble so that God is again evident.[9] Without judging either party's "things," in order for us to listen and be receptive, we need to make space for the other's "things," and therefore set our own aside. That does not mean we always respond gladly and we are never torn. It means we leave our own thoughts and feelings aside for the moment. They will keep. The moment will not. This is receptiveness.

What is it that the spiritual director gives? Open, willing receptiveness often translates into quantitative gifts of time, attention, and energy. These gifts are not quite ours, though. They flow through us. *Hineni* means giving what is given without a motive or expectations. It means giving without needs, without an agenda, from the God in me to the God in you, simply because the request is heard. That's all. Some call it grace.

Hineni calls for a bridging of the distance between director and directee, even as we do not fill it. When you do not fill in the emptiness, but let it remain empty, the other has the space to reveal him- or herself. As spiritual directors, we must dare to truly see, and then be willing for what we see to move us.

In those same Gospel stories (e.g., Matt 9:36; 20:29; Lk 7:13; Matt 15:32) in which Jesus is moved to his depths, we read that Jesus first sees—really sees—who is before him, allows space for the other to move him and then acts. Each time, he allows the moment to speak to him and does what the moment asks of him: he heals, comforts, and teaches. All of these actions occur after he went through his trial in the desert, and, like Abraham, went beyond himself.

Even so, there are times when we will feel inadequate to the task. "It is a feeling you never get over," one seasoned director remarked.

Sometimes, it is when we get to the end of our own capabilities and let go that something breaks and a different reality is revealed. Knowing this can make us more aware when the one before us has come to the end of his or her capability—verbal or otherwise—and can allow gentleness from the space, because of us, in spite of us.

The spiritual director sacrifices the need for reassurance, for certainty. Many are initially attracted toward spiritual direction because we are natural helpers. We eventually learn that our desire to help, as kind as it is, sometimes gets in the way. Letting go of wanting to get something out of it, letting go of the perspective of "I," is part of the willingness that is the sacrifice of *hineni*.

Abraham had to let go of Isaac so that he could become. God lets go of each of us so that we can do the same. This movement of *tzimtzum* is one which spiritual directors might do well to note. By resisting the urge to "help" the other, and, instead, letting go, we acknowledge that the other must travel his or her own path. Acknowledging the distance of otherness can become the space for divine encounter. Such "naked faith cannot be taught. Rather, it demands of each of us a personal confrontation." The only thing a spiritual director can offer is engaged withdrawal, which can be a challenging tension to hold in such an intimate relationship.[10] This sort of love is fundamentally sacrificial.

And yet, *hineni* is not about self-sacrifice. That space between verses 12 and 13 is about paying attention, in the moment, so that you can really see what is before you.[11] It is about putting your whole self in, which is not the same as its being about you. Putting your whole self in would seem to preclude guarding against consequences with walls around your heart. We do not get to hide.

Being fully present can also reveal a different way. Another translation of verse 14 reads: "In the space of God is the ability to see."[12]

Connection and Commitment

"Walking on together"—commitment and connection—happens when two or more share an experience, or when the other's truth is revealed in trust. It happens when one has heard the other's story, even if—perhaps especially when—it breaks his or her heart.

Responding is not without risk. Companioning the intimate journey of others can challenge what we think and believe and feel, shaking our own sense of comfort and safety, opening wounds we thought long closed. Being willing to be open and responsive does not guarantee what sort of response we will get.

Vulnerability entails a risk of failure. It means admitting we are imperfect and afraid, and yet not projecting that fear.[13] Sometimes, we won't notice the interruption; we are too busy to see. Or we are perhaps too full to really hear what the other is actually saying, which may not be the words at all.

There are also risks in balancing conflicting demands or competing commitments such as family and work. It is possible to be so wrapped up in responding to what we feel is our ultimate horizon, that we do not see the dangers—to ourselves or others—of the chosen path.[14]

While taping an interview for my study in spiritual direction, my son Josha, then fifteen, entered the room where I was working. I did not even look at him or address him. I just waved him away. He left, politely, without saying a word. When the taping was over, I noticed that he had slipped a note under my door, saying he had broken up with his girlfriend. My son was looking for love and consolation and I was too busy doing the work for a certificate in seeing the God in others to stop and see the one before me.

Real vulnerability in spiritual direction seems again related to that key sentence from the Gospels: Jesus was moved to his depths with compassion. Compassion is the place where connection and commitment meet. Compassion is not so much, "I am there for you" as "I am here with you." Compassion is full immersion in being human—in all its frailty, vulnerability, loneliness, and loss—all those things that leave us feeling inadequate and helpless.

Compassion, a form of lived *hineni*, is, like it, a beautiful but dangerous ideal. Besides the danger of burnout, getting into the habit of putting your own feelings and interests aside also poses a risk. You may eventually forget where you left them. A friend lived in a monastery in Rotterdam not one hundred meters from the famous statue by Zadkine, "The Destroyed City." The statue symbolizes Rotterdam, which had the heart bombed out of it in May of 1940. "I feel like the heart has been bombed out of me, too," he says, "after a lifetime of hearing problems and confessions and being a pastor to hundreds of people."

Vulnerability and compassion entail real risk, which means that there is no safe distance. While self-care and boundaries are essential (as the next chapter will show), there is no way to be present to people in compassion and guarantee your own safety. I am not saying that each spiritual director will wind up with a hole where his heart used to be. That, too, would be a formula. I am saying that it is possible. That is what risk means: no guarantees that you can be that compassionate and not break. Practicing spiritual direction with the presence that comes from seeing and being moved, from *hineni*, may not break or destroy us, but it will transform us.

Mystery and Oneness

Martin Buber defines faith as trusting in something without being able to give sufficient reason for that trust[15]— trusting in the mystery of what you do not know and probably never will. Such trust "cannot be possessed, but brings us into the vulnerable border area of God and self."[16] Paraphrasing Kushner, there is also, for the spiritual director, that gnawing suspicion that the mystery contains a hidden oneness. Part of the work of a spiritual director is to hold that tension, rather than resolving it. The late Rabbi Zalman Schachter-Shalomi said that a spiritual direction encounter is a moment of union. He prepared for it by recalling such a moment of his own. "To remember, helps to draw strength that is not ours, but comes from the One who deploys us."[17]

It is commonly held today that all that lives and is emerges from a fundamental oneness, whether you call it "pre–Big Bang," "God," or something else. Our childhood development mirrors that oneness. We emerge from the oneness with our mothers and live for a while in the childlike oneness that does not separate things out. Everything is connected and flows.[18] With distinguishing comes separateness, which reveals mystery; separateness allows relationship. Through relationship we can share, celebrate, and rediscover connection.

We do live our lives forward but understand them backward. Both director and directee are on a journey whose implications and impact cannot be foreseen. The ramifications even of responding to a simple request by saying *hineni* can be quite different from what either party imagined.

Awareness and Balance

Abraham's split—being pulled in two directions at once—is a reminder that need is endless. It is impossible to respond to everyone's need all the time. Jana Preble, a spiritual director with over fifty years of experience, remarked in a conversation, "When I leave what my inner being needs in order to survive, I am not present to myself. I cannot sustain presence constantly, without intervals of quiet. So, even though the need is endless, my energy is not."

Practically, there needs to be a balance between being there for the other and the kind of self-care from which being there can flow. It would seem to be a moment-by-moment balance between knowing what your limits are and yet not having your limits become barriers to responding in the moment. So, unconditional, but with conditions.

Of course, there are times, like mine with my son, when each of us is so engrossed in the "work of God" that we miss the moment. Even Martin Buber, who understood what I-Thou means and taught that meaning to the rest of us, was not immune.

> Martin Buber was working, absorbed in his own thoughts, when a student knocked at his door. Buber was known as a wise counselor to young, seeking souls. He did not know Mehe, the young man at the door, but the professor invited the student in. Buber was not a rude man. He listened politely, but his mind and heart were elsewhere. He did not discern the true nature of Mehe's visit.
>
> Two months later, a friend of Mehe's came to see Buber, to tell him that Mehe had died. He also told Buber what Mehe had hoped the talk would have been. Mehe

had not come for a chat, but for help with a decision—one of life and death.

Buber was devastated. Mehe had come out of deepest need and Buber was too absorbed in his own thoughts and world to truly see.

Buber's life was changed forever by this encounter. As a result, he wrote *I and Thou*. His life and philosophy were permanently redirected because of how he had failed to respond. His seminal work had no point if he failed to be truly present to those before him.[19]

Direction in the Moment

Hineni, as we noted at the beginning of the book, translates inadequately into "Here I am." In other words, where we are now is where we need to be. The journey gives us the opportunity to hear the call and respond. The journey is the point. We are already here.

Hineni is about "letting go of preconceived ideas and gently bringing ourselves into the presence of what is—not what we imagine or remember or desire. To be truly present requires conscious, sustained effort and attention, and a willingness to be authentic, awake and attuned."[20]

Being and becoming is the process that both director and directee undergo as they participate in the relationship. As Augustine noted, we are made *toward* God. That is the direction of spiritual direction. The imitation of Abraham is not about doing the same as Abraham did. Rather, it is about going in a direction, toward who each of us is beyond narrative. The God of Abraham, the God of Isaac, and the God of Israel must *become* our God, too.

III

Collected Wisdom from the Field

Introduction

Spiritual directors need guidance, too, in order to become who we are in the depth of us. We need others to look over our shoulders, reminding us to pay attention, noting the ditches on the sides of our road. We need people who will lift up our broken shards to the light. Those who have gone before us and those who engage with us as living examples help us grow and develop in ways we could not do without them. They, too, say *hineni*.

In this chapter, eight spiritual directors, representing over 250 years of experience, will share their wisdom of lived *hineni*. In imitation of Abraham, each has found his or her own way to make the Name. Each unique example adds to the wisdom tradition for those of us who come after them. Consider them markings for the way.

Six (Pippa and I excluded) were sent a questionnaire. In order not to have the respondents get stuck on a word which might not have been familiar to them, after *hineni* was defined, the word *presence* was substituted. The following narratives have been fashioned from the questionnaire responses.

Open for Encounter: Rabbi Awraham Soetendorp

Awraham was born in 1943 in Amsterdam, the Netherlands, in the middle of World War II. When he was still an infant, his father, himself a rabbi, brought him to Amsterdam Central Station in a suitcase, where he was picked up and saved by a righteous Catholic couple. Ordained in 1967, he was instrumental in the reestablishment of Jewish communities in the Netherlands. Awraham is the founder and/or leader of many social-justice groups on national and international levels, including the Jacob Soetendorp Institute for Human Values, Green Cross International, and the Day of Respect Foundation.

"Where there is a surprise in the moment, you're open. For me, there is a joy in encounter because I know that, whatever the combination of people, there is always something new. When you go on a journey, you plan your journey in some detail, but you know that, after the journey, you will discover there was something unplanned or unexpected, that was maybe more important than all the planning . . . ."

For Awraham, spontaneity, being utterly in the moment, is key to *hineni*, so he neither plans nor prepares before an encounter, other than maintaining the paradoxical awareness that, when he enters a space with another, something unique happens, and there is no preparing for that.

Awraham uses the *Amida*, the prayer central in Jewish daily prayers, to illustrate: "At the end of the *Amida*, there is a prayer for peace, after which you retreat three steps and then come back three steps. Retreating three steps means you create space for peace. In order to create space you have to retreat, and only then you can come back. So, there is also a moment in which you have retreat to yourself to allow that space for the other."

Being fully in the moment also means that Awraham doesn't "have to know a lot about the person who comes." Nor does he even want to know, because what is essential will become clear in the questions. "The only 'plan,' if you can call it that, is the hope that the person who comes into my room will leave lighter. There is no magic, but there is an opportunity.

"Coincidence plays an important role in all of this, and there are always coincidences. And coincidences are the moment you become aware of the fact that there is a cosmic order of which you are a part. Einstein said that coincidence is G'd's way of remaining anonymous—that reference always makes people smile." He recalls one such coincidence:

"One day, I came out of my office after a meeting. In the other room there was a group of people learning Hebrew. I was struck by a person who was wandering about, eyes shifting, we sat down, then he suddenly started to tell me how terrible his life was.

"I was listening, not prepared, and had no prior relationship with him. Suddenly, I felt a word, and I answered with that word. He looked at me, shaken, and he said, 'That's it! That is the key to the problem I have been struggling with for 20 years.' I don't know what happened after that. He disappeared from my life. I see this (encounter) as a product of the fact that I was completely unprepared and open to sudden words and associations."

Of course, there are costs, risks, and down sides of being present. Over the course of fifty years, the list is long.

Being present to encounter has sometimes meant being absent to his family, particularly to his wife, not having time even to read a book or just to do nothing. "Maybe [I have sacrificed] my love for arts, for writing and literature and my love of theater. I have chosen my path in life, and that world is still open to me, but I would have liked to have lived both lives to the full."

Being fully in the moment means that pre-set boundaries feel artificial to him. Not having boundaries entails risk, and Awraham is aware of this. Yet—and his experience bears this out—the struggle that can present itself within the risk of vulnerability, might reveal boundaries inherent to the moment.

Presence, for Awraham, also means putting his whole self in: "The only existential way to meet the other is in his or her otherness, and to allow that otherness to be in dialogue with yourself." Just as with spontaneity, this aspect of presence carries with it potential hazards or extremes. Awraham refers to Levinas, who pointed out the danger that you might overpower the other, almost forcing them to be a carbon copy follower of your own way.

There is also the danger you might be so subservient, that you only see the position of the other, thereby losing the perspective you could be adding to the whole.

Acknowledging these extremes, Awraham adds one of his own. Creating space in order to receive the story of another entails creating an atmosphere of safety, which he does by sharing from his own experience. Invariably, this means he sometimes shares too much and is too present. He hopes that awareness means he self-corrects.

Smugness—the feeling that "I have done it"—is a constant struggle for him. "When a meeting is finished and I feel delighted, I struggle, because I feel that the delight should be in what we both achieved together, but not in my ability and what I added. I am an instrument."

Spiritual guidance is also deeply personal and feelings are definitely in play. Awraham sketches two possible polar scenarios: "One, a situation where somebody whom I tried to help, and I know that I invested a lot in, and the person is very angry at me years later—as if I had done nothing at all. I find this very difficult to cope with, because I will never say 'but you know what I did' and yet the person speaks only about what I did not do.

"The other situation is that a person comes to me and says, 'We have not seen each other for a long time, but I'm so grateful for what you did for me'—and I really did not know what I did, and the person did not believe that. That I have had moments when I really did not know that, or in what way, I helped the other person, those are cherished moments."

There is no safe distance in real presence. Awraham shares this story: "A woman was in a depression and had to be taken to a psychiatric ward. It was the weekend, and she could not find a doctor to help her. She left the room, and I did not want her to leave, so I tried to reach the psychiatrist. I gave her his telephone number. When I came home, I was restless, and called the psychiatrist and called again. I could not find him, and she committed suicide. This is buried in my consciousness."

Awraham admits he has never been able to completely liberate himself from anxiety. He has sought professional help for it and been advised, "Despite the experience that you have, if someone wants to take his life, he will do it. You have to overcome this."

He sought help another time, only to wind up being the helper. The relationship became unhealthy and led to a near-addiction. Being open and willing, in the moment, to the one before you is never without risk.

Even with these hazards, being present as his "whole self" is a risk that Awraham feels he must take. It allows "relationships between oneself, other people, other cultures, other life, and the larger whole(ness) of which all are part." It is, he adds, the way of peace.

So, what does "your whole self" look like for Awraham? Well, it means warmth, walking into a room with a smile, and offering a hug or handshake. The main quality he brings, although he is quick to qualify this by saying it is not a method or formula, is simply "being a *Mensch*, listening and speaking with your heart, without leaving your intellect behind." It includes sharing, being vulnerable, and loving.

The detachment he was taught at rabbinical school does not work for him. The sense of connection he has felt toward those he encounters, expresses itself in engaged commitment. It matters to him when someone leaves angry, in tears, or not feeling "a little lighter." He has tried to manage his involvement, to let people go, knowing that he cannot take away all the anxieties from all people. "I have to keep my sanity," he acknowledges, "but I think that the other way, of going home and leaving all your sorrows and joy behind, is [also] not a solution."

Awraham adds that "all qualities have two sides: water is essential to life, but can bring disaster, as with a flood. It is the same with fire, or religious fervor: full of warmth, or positive embrace, but both can also kill. Still, I think that authenticity is never a hindrance."

Authenticity also means that Awraham is a rabbi on the street, where he wears a *kippah*, even though it is not required of liberal (Reform) Jews. He's done this ever since he returned from the Soviet Union to Holland with a planeload of Jewish refugees. He did not want to hide the fact that he was Jewish, but he had no idea what it would do to him.

On the surface, wearing it tended to get him into trouble. Wearing it while accompanying journalists and politicians to Jericho, placed him on the wrong end of a gun. The man holding it turned out to be a member of the Palestinian police, there to protect him. Wearing it during a television interview offended other progressive rabbis, because, with it, he seemed to represent the orthodox branch of the religion, instead of his own. Yet it mostly works to narrow the gaps within that larger identity, too. It is a constant reminder of who he wants to be, and who he is in his core, sometimes laying bare inner tension with daily reality. So, what started out as an act of almost defiant identity, has worked to bring greater inner wholeness and outer oneness. Authenticity.

Authenticity means he is also a rabbi each time he enters a room. It also means an awareness of his—and everyone else's —uniqueness and the mystery of that uniqueness. The respect that emerges from this awareness engenders openness, willingness, and desire for connection. It has also resulted in some highly unusual encounters: blessing an atheist, giving the blessing of Aaron over a Hindu teacher at the Parliament of World Religions, and praying for, and then with, Pope Francis.

He has learned that sometimes it is a blessing to others to let them bless you, and that, by letting that happen, both are truly blessed. Letting it happen, rather than sticking to the roles in the script, is one of those surprises or coincidences he is open for, and he urges others to be as well.

He has made mistakes. This is inevitable. He always hopes that an apology will be accepted and that the relationship can continue. He carries the wisdom of forgiveness, expressed in the mystical ideas of Adin Steinsaltz: "You can't change the past, but you can learn from it. You can learn from your mistakes so that they can become a powerful force for changing the future."

Finally, presence for Awraham is not so much a practice as it is life: "I think that, in some way, everything is spiritual. That is why we have a spirit. Spirit sustains us . . . . My mother taught me that 'We talk to each other in silence.' Breath [*ruach*, spirit] is important in meditation, but being conscious of breath is difficult for me, because it can hamper spontaneity.

"It is very important to learn the lesson, also within Judaism, that sacred and profane are not completely separated. There is a flow, just as there is no good and evil in absolute terms, so you have to discern.

"So there are the rays of light amid the darkness, and darkness amid the rays of light. I think (the totality of) it adds to our lives.

[To be present] is also about feeding yourself. In Judaism we say that when you are at a table, you should not leave it without a word of Torah spoken. It is a very good directive, because it allows you to say, 'I read from a book, or gave a lesson.' But it can also mean that there is something worthwhile happening. You eat your bread, you touch a hand, you share. So the table is also an altar—even if it is at a coffee shop."

Mysticism at Street Level: Leo Raphael de Jong, OP

Leo is a Dominican friar. He has been a priest, pastor, and spiritual director for individuals and groups for about sixty years. He has degrees in church history and theology, as well as extensive training in spiritual direction and spirituality. Decades of profession have moved him "beyond denominations," including the Roman Catholic one he still serves. He is deeply embedded in the spirituality of Rhineland Mysticism and the teachings of his Dominican forebear and brother, Meister Eckhart.

The tension between empty space and spacious emptiness is the core of Leo's spirituality and the point of departure for his practice of spiritual direction.

Leo describes this as a movement between emptiness, which means no certainty, no beliefs, no longer knowing, even the feeling of being worthless and lost, and space, in which he enjoys the room to doubt, sees guilt as unimportant; the room simply to be, of being carried, of surrender. "The most important thing for me, in making space to be present for the other, is that I am in contact with my own depth, the abyss of not knowing. I do this through the knowledge and practice of Rhineland Mysticism."

Emptiness—open, willing receptiveness, waiting in stillness—is also one of the most important personal qualities Leo brings to his directees. From the altar, Leo still listens attentively to the readings and prayers, open to movements that will inform his sermons, which are written with "spaces" in them, just in case. Leo prepares his environment, often lighting a candle in front of an icon before the start of a course or a session with a directee.

Being attentive to God is Leo's core business as a monk. He practices objectless meditation—meditation without an object of focus. In itself, this is a practice in open awareness. Such a practice does not produce immediate results, but after a while one notices a difference. There is a difference, Leo notes, when he does not do it. He calls himself a "professional seeker of God" and is attentive to that journey into the interior.

Daily practice and attentiveness help Leo remain open to interruptions, and, as he notes, "There have been times when someone came to my door, totally unexpected, and asked for my help. Such breaking in sometimes wound up being a source of new and deeper spiritual insight and contact for me, too."

Much of Leo's spiritual direction now has to do with "awakening the master in the one before me." This is the purpose of his work. He seeks ways to "strengthen the directee's feeling about God, also by using texts of the mystics." As the directee's own mastership awakens, Leo "seeks to stimulate, question and reinforce." He trains hearts to see.

Leo notes that the practice of presence begins by letting any appointments he makes emerge from the directee, from their calling *ayekah*, where are you? His feelings about any person or group play no role in the process. Similarly, he tries to leave his own work and worries "in the fridge," so that he can approach the other(s) as empty as possible.

Leo came by emptiness honestly, as a result of a spiritual crisis in 1972. He had been a priest for about ten years:

> During training in pastoral skills, something, some feeling, overwhelmed me. Though I was wide awake and it was early morning, I "dreamed" that I was in a deep, slippery well. I tried to climb up the walls to get out of the pit, but I kept sliding back. It seemed better to sink into the well, all the way down, in hope of getting to the bottom and finding some solid ground which would help me to free myself. But the solid ground was not there. I fell through the mud and ended up in a dark, swirling, cold nothing, in a void.
>
> All the ground on which I stood, all certainties, which were the foundations of my life, fell away from me. Certainties, like my belief in myself and in my functioning as

a human being and as a priest; the answer to the question whether I was a good person; my Catholic faith with its bible, dogmas and morality; even my choice to remain a member of the order of the Dominicans. In short, my belief in everything on which my life was founded, slipped away. It felt like I was left in an infinite, swirling, slippery darkness.

It was a tremendously shocking experience and took me months to find my footing again, even though, on the surface, I continued with my work.

Only after a few years had passed did Leo discover that others had had experiences like his own, experiences described in the long history of Rhineland Mysticism. No one had ever taught him about that. At the time, mysticism was considered a form of escapism, if it was seen at all. He teaches about it now in courses around the general topic "Mysticism at Street Level"—mysticism in everyday ordinary life today.

Despite decades of experience, Leo still can feel inadequate to the task: "Who am I to be guiding another on their spiritual path, a path that is even hazy to them?" That question does not go away. "In the moment, I do the best I can. Afterwards, I am quite aware that my actions were far from great. This, too, I have to let go. The rest is the way of the other and I have looked with him, as best I could."

For better or worse, Leo brings his whole self to a session, which can make things more personal, because his own insights and experiences can also be tools, as long as he remains aware of what is his. Sometimes, he notices that he is "too busy teaching about what is important to me—the mystagogue in me gets the upper hand." And sometimes, he is just too preoccupied to be truly present to the other. Emptiness, he notes, is both a gift and a task.

Boundaries for Leo are not rigid, but rather guides to be applied flexibly. He tries to limit time, because such intimate talks make both parties tired, and he seeks a balance between "optimal distance and optimal engagement," even if the ideal is elusive. He confesses to being better at engagement than distance, and while he does not perceive this as a hindrance, it has caused some problems.

Both words and gestures can be openings for greater insight into the way of a directee, Leo has learned. Reacting in the moment makes both vulnerable, exactly because the other might not realize what is being revealed, and a question or observation can push buttons. Some directees lash out as a result, and then—as always—it is important to trust in the deep stillness.

Hineni as being in the moment emerges from Leo's retrospective look at his practice. Looking back, he observes that, decades ago, he was in that "now," complete with those insights and that knowledge and that capability. Now, he is in this "now," with what he has to bring to it. Better? Worse? He does not know and is not sure it really matters.

Steeped in Oneness: Blanche Bunting, OSB

Blanche (not her real name) has been a sister in the Order of Saint Benedict for sixty-two years. In addition to being a spiritual director with thirteen years of experience, she is the coordinator of volunteers at the monastery's Spirituality Center. She also tends to elements in and around the center that add beauty and interest for the guests.

"Being attentive to God is my life and I love it! I would not give it up for anything!" Blanche describes a life steeped in a sense of oneness. "God is present everywhere and in everything. I cannot and do not want it to be different. All that is, is one, and I am connected to all of creation . . . my sleeping, waking, sunrise and set, smiles, voices, birds, friends, sorrows, joys, deaths and illness, doing dishes, praying with and without community. God is in all of this."

Maintaining presence expresses Blanche's sense of oneness. Centering Prayer helps her to be present in daily life. "Being thoughtful and not rushing in my walking and working" contributes to an overall awareness.

"Presence is the basis for my ability to truly listen to the spoken word of the deep mystery that lies within each directee," Blanche says. "Only if I am present, am I able to listen to what is said and what is not said.

"My spiritual life is about noticing and listening to the messages of God that I encounter every day. If I listen, I can hear God's voice in the beauty of creation, the events of my life, the joys and sufferings, and the ordinary times of my day. I was told that, as a spiritual director, my first role was to be a listener. I think this means that I must be attentive to the movement of God in directees and in my own heart as I direct others."

Even though she has felt inadequate during some sessions, and knows she cannot always maintain presence within a session, Blanche has learned that she is "not the important one in any session. All of spiritual direction is the work of God, the loving Spirit in the life of this one, precious child of God sitting in front of me. I am an instrument in the hands of God—not just in spiritual direction, but also in my life. I pray daily for those I journey with, that I be given wisdom, understanding and discernment in my sessions with them."

Intent and desire play an important part in her practice. Blanche creates space, both mental and physical, for her directees. Half of her office is set aside for spiritual direction. She keeps that space simple, inviting, and peaceful. Before a directee arrives, she tries to put aside what she is doing. Preparation includes prayer, Scripture reading, and reflection on the directee's last session, noting where they seem to be in their relationship with God.

Blanche sometimes writes poetry to awaken whatever is needed in her mind and heart, and to help her remember her sacred calling.

Preparing to Listen
With this quiet moment of time
I hope to blot out all distractions
and the busy signals in my mind.
I await your coming into
the space of this room
and hold you up in prayer.

I pray the flame of this lit candle
will light the fire in my soul
and unite it with God's gift
of gracious wisdom and
discernment.

May I not interfere in your
dialogue with God, but help
make the dialogue happen,
so that you may listen
like Mary, and respond
from your heart.
Amen.

Making people feel comfortable and safe are gifts that Blanche brings to her practice. Cultivated awareness is another. Years of experience in the healthcare field and her way of life have also provided some helpful qualities. "[My work] helped me to be more compassionate, aware of the aging process and suffering." She also grew to see "the value and importance of the spiritual life when confronted with difficulties and challenges."

To be aware of surrendering to the love of God into greater freedom, both for herself and her directees, is a process. "I need to remind myself to let go of control and allow God to teach the directee in God's good time, not mine. I need to watch any tendency to want to fix, solve, or avoid. Becoming aware of my issues is key to being watchful during sessions."

Boundaries make it easier for Blanche to journey with directees. They help her "forget about basic concerns that might otherwise arise" in the course of the relationship. She sets boundaries in a gentle way during the first session. These include the frequency of sessions, time limits, cancellation policies, confidentiality, and the professional nature of the relationship. There may be others specific to an individual.

Blanche believes directees need freedom to stay, leave, or do whatever they need to do on their journey to God. This does not mean that another's taking that freedom is not sometimes disappointing. Blanche participates in regular peer supervision, where such feelings and experiences are examined. She also has her own spiritual director and a sister at the Spirituality Center, with whom to talk things through.

"Journeying with others," says Blanche, "is a privilege; it is sacred time." She sees most of spiritual direction as service: "blessing and not sacrifice." If she needs to give up time to fit a schedule, she hopes she does so "with generosity and grace."

"I believe God gives me directees for a reason," Blanche notes. So it really is mutual. "I am learning all the time. . . . Presence is hard to describe," she concludes, "but it has to do with a loving look at the real in any situation. I am human. I do my best, and leave the rest up to God."

Increasing Independence: Rev. Peter Korver

Peter is a Protestant minister with thirty years of experience as a spiritual director. He taught high school for many years as well. Peter studied spiritual direction at the Titus Brandsma Institute for Spirituality in Nijmegen and wrote his final thesis on "Talking about God."

"The word 'God' does not have to be spoken for the encounter to be about what is essential." In other words, in order to talk about God, you do not have to talk about God. Peter brings this non-judgmental, open and listening attitude to his practice.

Talking about essential matters, however, requires vigilance.

First, there needs to be an awareness of God. For Peter, this means a regular prayer life, moments of quiet meditation so he can become free of thoughts. God is the "third person" in every encounter. It means awareness of God through biblical (and other) texts. His trust in God, he notes, gives a sense of trust and confidence to the other in a direction session.

Second, Peter is vigilant regarding himself. Restlessness, impatience, or sleepiness serve as signals that his attention may be wandering. These can also be signs that he is not maintaining presence to himself or attending to his inner life. It is difficult to listen to another when you are burdened yourself, and a spiritual director, or a pastor, is only human. Peter is not always able to give.

Third, Peter is acutely aware of interpersonal dynamics. Presence to the one before him means, "Here I am, now, for you, with all my attention and compassion." Those who come are usually "glad that someone gives time and listens with attention." He is alert not to be carried away by the emotions of a directee, even though he may be touched. Instead of delving into everything that is expressed, Peter sticks to naming only what he sees and hears.

"Trying to summarize, analyze or find a solution" are signals for Peter that he is "too present." It is all about awareness. "It is part of a professional attitude that you are always critical of yourself."

"Sometimes the story of another seems similar to my own. And then I must be particularly aware" not to project. Furthermore, Peter acknowledges that he carries a professional "deformity": "All that attention to the questions and cares of others, not asking for attention myself, has become an attitude I bring to relationships with friends and family as well."

Boundaries are clear and help Peter maintain presence. Sessions take place in his home and are limited to a maximum of two hours. No calls after 9:00 p.m., and he prefers to keep his personal life personal. Perhaps most importantly, the directee must take responsibility for his or her own journey, must not become dependent on the director, so that the director "does not become overburdened or drained." Signs of dependence include often asking for advice or excessive contact between sessions. "Spiritual direction should increase the independence" of the directee.

Finally, Peter feels that a pastor must always be ready to put his other work aside when someone calls out in need, "Like a monastic learns to stop his work immediately when the bell rings for prayer. . . . It is surprising how unimportant important things actually are in the light of someone else's concerns. Being open teaches you to see the relativity of many things."

Responding in God: Jana Preble

Jana is a spiritual director, professor emerita of psychology, consultant, Benedictine oblate, wife, mother, and grandmother. She has over fifty years of experience as a spiritual director and is a welcome asset to the Benedictine—and wider—community that she serves. Her research included assisting Viktor Frankl and Elisabeth Lukas by extending logotherapy research from Europe to include North American studies.

"Presence . . . is the fundamental offering of the director to the directee—to be mindful and open and receptive to the mystery of God within and surrounding both of us. It is the heart of the relationship. . . . Presence does not so much play a role; rather, it embodies the reality of God's presence already given." Jana describes presence as a core mutuality in the direction relationship. As she offers presence, she is "filled with wonder at God's presence revealed" in the one before her.

Jana *practices* presence. Connection is embodied in every aspect of her life: in prayer; with her family, friends, and directees; in the sacraments, songs, and community; in nature, listening, reading, holding hands, and gazing into another's eyes. Faithfulness to practices—prayer, *lectio divina*, contemplative practice—as well as balance between work and leisure, with adequate time for quiet and social engagement, help her maintain presence and balance. She considers these helps "foundational to my being." Without them, she notes, she becomes "fatigued, distracted, agitated or (rarely) bored."

While awareness of connection is central for Jana, she admits that "being attentive to God is a full-time commitment that is sometimes poorly realized. Since God is in every event, in every place, in every person and creature, one's mind invariably wanders from the source at times. I think we are meant to be distracted by all of these and not meant to *think* about God so much as to *respond in* God."

In a session, Jana is rarely distracted. Her attention is focused in two places at once: "on the directee—on every aspect—mind, body, emotion, eyes," and on "God's love for them, God's work in their lives. My attention is focused (in these ways) because my undying stance is that God the Holy Spirit is the Director. I am an attendant."

Although Jana is not easily distracted, "interruptions have been a way of life for me since childhood. Generally, they arrive as a surprise at times when life seems to be peaceful and absorbing. Many have been life-changing. Whether I have been initially open or not, the interruptions ultimately seem to have their way."

An "interruption" moved her from her peaceful domestic life, which included informal spiritual companionship to those who sought her out, to the professional role she still enjoys today. Her husband, an Episcopal priest, brought her a brochure describing a study in Christian spirituality. Despite her initial protests, he persisted. "The interruption of a small brochure, a big nudge from my husband and the Holy Spirit combined to form a life that continues to move forward in ways I cannot predict." The surprise element has not faded. "Unexpected and inconvenient interruptions arriving daily can be full of fruitful potential."

Still, there are times when Jana does not feel like opening the door to an unexpected caller.

"If the resistance prevails, I sometimes feel disappointed in myself, sorry for my lack of openness. At other times, I realize that sometimes, resistance is necessary so that I can recover from too many activities or too much engagement. The question is, when is the closed door necessary so that

I can regain perspective enough to be open, and when is it simply stubborn selfishness?"

Jana has "a strong conviction that God is love and that God loves this person no matter what. I trust in the Holy Spirit's guidance—for both of us."

"Quiet receptivity allows openness and space; an invitation for whatever the directee might bring." The conviction that God is love and loves the directee unconditionally "gives me the confidence to offer reassurance of that love repeatedly. Patience allows me to wait for whatever the directee may bring to be revealed. Spiritual direction is a process, a journey. I've never regretted being patient, but I can be and need to be assertive, too, at times."

Encouragement sometimes complements her willingness to wait, and "listening is most of what I do. I listen to the person; I listen for the guidance of the Holy Spirit." Jana feels that this guidance is her constant companion. The gifts of the Holy Spirit "act as touchstones or indicators" of what she watches for in a directee. In addition, body language and facial expression are keys in her understanding of emotional content.

Openness means vulnerability. Sometimes, this means feeling sorry as Jana sees a directee make what she feels to be a destructive choice for him- or herself. As difficult as it is, her boundaries make clear that the choice is the directee's to make, not hers.

Jana is in the position of being a spiritual director to people in the community she worships with, so rigid boundaries are neither possible nor advisable. Usually, her directees know her "to some degree before they choose to come for spiritual direction." Still, the session is the session: prayer, quiet, openness and privacy set the boundaries. She is clear that directees should leave matters of spiritual direction for sessions, rather than bring them into outside encounters with her. Some of her directees are themselves directors, so "this kind of fluid relationship does not pose a problem."

"The boundaries of the session open the door for the directee to speak of anything at all that is on their heart. Sometimes encountering directees within the context of their lives is a help to being present to them in a session." Still, Jana is careful to keep her responses in a session to what the directee is saying in the here and now: "Here we are together in this relationship; what you bring at this time is what I want to receive."

Jana knows the shadow side of presence. "It is God whom I rely on for me to be attentive in whatever manner of being I bring to the moments of life. Attentiveness is God's action and gift, too—hanging on to control of attention is not always the way of loving attentiveness."

Time and spontaneity are sacrifices Jana is aware of making in order to serve in the way she does.

"I often relinquish my preferred daily schedule in order to fit my directees' needs. I give up time that I would enjoy spending in other ways even though I enjoy spiritual direction and directees. The giving up of time is the largest sacrifice, together with the consequent missing of other events/

opportunities/joys that I am not available for when I have spiritual direction appointments. Spontaneous availability is sacrificed to the schedule of appointments."

"Sometimes," Jana observes, "people are so caught up in the myriad details of living that they wonder where God is in all of it. This is human, I think, normal for most. People have been attentive to God for me and I am grateful. For others, it depends on each person—one way doesn't work for all. But it always comes down to love—drawing on the awareness of the gifts of love."

God's Story in Them: Hein Blommestijn, OCarm

Hein is a Carmelite and Catholic priest. He holds degrees in psychology and spirituality and has been a professor of mystical theology. He is a writer and academic researcher in the fields of mysticism and spirituality. He has been a spiritual director for "50 years more or less." At the Titus Brandsma Institute, Hein's lectures were characterized by a sense of presence, conveying something beyond the content.

"Even if the person in front of me seems understandable, this is only a projection. Therefore, there is no real difference between the person who tells a 'rational story' and the person who speaks in a very enigmatic or even strange way. In both cases, I will have to listen to the person 'behind' the obviously present person."

A vigilant awareness is key to Hein's sense of presence. "This is only possible," he says, "if I become open to the divine reality in the person from the perspective of the divine reality in myself. This is not a single and easy step, but an ongoing process, because anxiety and uncertainty seduce me continuously to reduce the person to my idea or to construct a theory about him or her (a kind of diagnosis). I have to go back to the mystery present in front of me and ask God to reveal to me his idea about this person, to pray, listen and contemplate in order to see the person seen and loved by God."

An interruption by ill health left Hein with a strong awareness that his whole life is pure grace and does not belong to him, but "He lives in me." No more, no less. He looks back on such interruptions as gifts. There are sometimes encounters with others who find themselves in impossible situations, confronting Hein with his own incapacity. "Then, I am forced to be endlessly patient, leaving to God his solution, which I do not know."

Prayer and contemplation are central to his being and practice. Hein listens to the word spoken to him personally by God in this moment, in this situation, in this person or these people. His is a "life of prayer and continuously contemplating all of reality around, without any theory." He also writes poetry "as a way of seeing what is invisible." He listens, without understanding, knowing he does not understand, "waiting for what might happen in the other, without the possibility of speeding it up or offering possible solutions, without even the possibility of helping the other to understand himself."

So, even after fifty years, he still can feel inadequate. Waiting and patience and openness are the qualities he brings, which serve both the directee and the director. "Just waiting and being kind, not pushing in any way" has sometimes meant that the other has "felt understood and slowly made some steps."

Hein is very aware of perspective, and those times when it can shift or has shifted to "I." He recalls times when he imagined a future for a directee (that did not work, he readily admits), or became bored by the story being told. While each represents a very different level of activity, in both cases, he was "able to come back to the center."

Hein addresses the need for limits and boundaries very clearly.

Boundaries "help to be present in a real way and not to remain kind in a useless way." He does not accept a directee, for example, who "shuns the disturbing and painful confrontation with God," preferring to "stick to common spirituality and piety." Getting bored and sleepy are for him physical signals that the directee is becoming more self-centered and escaping that confrontation.

Furthermore, he is keenly aware of attempts by the other to manipulate him in order not to change. As soon as he notices such behavior, the direction ends. This is "an abuse of his time and energy in a useless way." Despite fifty years of practice, such treatment can still feel hurtful or disappointing.

Being willing to be vulnerable means that Hein's foundations are regularly shaken.

"Real confrontation with God brings us into a desert and provokes unbearable anxiety. I am terribly 'maladjusted' to God—a sinner compared to God's holiness. Accompanying deep anxiety (Dark Night) in others confronts me with the inevitable deep anxiety in myself. Encountering God, not as an idea or a concept, [but] really in person, inevitably provokes a deep anxiety. This is not a problem to be solved, but has to be understood, respected and accepted as the only reality which exists. We cannot escape God. Most 'religion' is more of a tranquilizer or a form of anesthetic, therefore a compromise for a more 'human' god, a soft projection."

What does Hein know now that he wishes he had known earlier? Reading the mystics promotes insights that remain ever new.

All is grace. For Hein, this means that "at any moment, and in each situation, I can discover the (hidden) presence of God—listening to the song of a bird, looking at the waves in the sea . . . and discovering the face of God, his presence, in the face of every person—though this requires patience and a lot of respect." Always, just as he teaches his students, he is listening for the story behind the story, mostly hidden, even from the directee—that is God's story.

Love on Four Legs: Pippa Labrador

Pippa is a Black Labrador Retriever, now twelve years old. She has been practicing her own unique form of spiritual direction her whole life. On the streets of Kralingen, she regularly sniffs out people who seem to need a bit of extra love. Her current work brings her to Pniël, a care facility in her neighborhood.

Pippa reflects a part of God to her world. Love is the gift she brings to her practice. Being filled with love leaves no room for feelings of inadequacy. She loves the world without a reason for it and without judging and finds the joy in everything. Pippa has a great gift for seeing straight to the heart of the one before her, to the God in them.

Presence is inherent to her being. Awareness and nowness are natural outgrowths of that presence. "Now I put my soft, wet nose into this man's dangling hand." The man's lifeless face lights up: "It took a dog to remind me that I am human." With her warm, brown eyes, she "looks compassion on the world." "Hey," said the homeless man selling papers, "your dog is trying to get your attention, and she is asking me to help her."

Pippa is not aware of setting any boundaries. Even a leash is less limit than connection—a means for pulling the one at the other end toward the next encounter. She is open, receptive, and willing. When she was a puppy, she was sometimes too present and knocked people over with her enthusiasm. She knows better now. Because she is so attuned to the moment, she can sense needs and respond to them without words. Her head on a knee has brought tears and evoked stories that seemed to need telling. She often listens and observes, head tilted to one side, without commenting or interrupting.

Trust is second nature for Pippa. Total dependence is not a matter of shame for her, but a way of living that trust. Serving is not a sacrifice, but as natural as breath. She submits readily to what is asked of her, without question. Occasionally, the reaction from the other side is not what she expected. She just tries harder.

Similarly, there are no interruptions for Pippa. She lets come what comes. The resulting encounter always brings something new: new smells, a pat on the head, soft-sounding words, a playmate—and sometimes a treat.

Pippa engenders community. Others who know her, take delight in her. The first time she carried meat home in her mouth, the butcher ran outside with his camera to capture the milestone. In the shop, they, too, had been waiting for that rite of passage.

Pippa shares some valuable lessons: "Finding a purpose beyond myself makes life truly rich. Sometimes we need reminding that we are not in control. Live life in the present and be alert to unexpected pleasures and opportunities. It takes patience and hard work to become who we are truly meant to be."[1]

The Story as the Story:
Hineni and People Living with Dementia

It is now my turn to share, not expertise, but, on a very practical level, what my work has taught me about *hineni* and people living with dementia. For them, the nowness of *hineni* seems particularly essential, because ideas of past and future are often blurred.

Practically, the specific challenge here is how to companion people with whom connection through language is not always self-evident, so that they can sense meaning, be respected, and maintain dignity and integrity. People with dementia are more present than is commonly assumed. One just must be willing to enter a different reality.

The world of dementia has acted as a crucible for me as a spiritual director. There is no fixing dementia, and so any such tendencies on my part are quickly thwarted. *Hineni* on the ward needs to be unadorned, authentic. Although comfort and reassurance are sometimes welcome and appropriate, the most important gifts to offer are a safe place to have feelings heard and a genuine willingness to acknowledge another's wholeness and receive their reality. That reality includes pain, being afraid, feeling alone or isolated, and dreading having no say in what happens to them.

People like to tell their stories. Stories anchor and comfort them. The willingness to receive them without interpretation is important. Sometimes, the story is a confession or a way to express unresolved grief. It may be possible to address individual concerns, but only if the reality is affirmed first.

I have also learned the hard way that the truth of *hineni* is beyond results and beyond feelings of self-satisfaction. Those with dementia reveal a terrifying reality of love. In each of them, God is becoming senile, just as in Jesus, God died on the cross. The challenge then becomes God needing compassion and love. Can I give it? The following is an example of what it is like for me on the ward:

Mrs. S. was, by any measure, a handful. She complained all the time. She was demanding and insistent. Her daughter had had enough long ago. She told me so, and yet she came to visit, loyally and regularly. The staff members were short with Mrs. S. They needed to be, to protect themselves from her incessant demands and criticism. Their brusqueness was sometimes shocking to me, but then I swoop in every week for two hours and swoop back out. I do not dwell in the endlessness of their work for forty hours a week.

One Thursday afternoon, Mrs. S. was particularly demanding. She was in pain. The process of sitting down was painful, so she had decided to remain standing until the next time she was taken to the bathroom. In two hours. I forgot to mention that she was also stubborn, and that she bothered the staff so much to take her to the bathroom that they actually wrote a schedule for her—every two hours— and checked it off each time.

The staff had given up trying to get her to sit. It took me twenty minutes of patient reasoning with her—twenty minutes the staff did not have—to finally get her to sit. She spent the next two hours complaining to me. And for those two hours, I listened. Of course, I was not good enough, either. We all knew that was coming. It was not pleasant. Pleasant is gratifying.

Then my shift, and Pippa's, was up. I stood to leave. There was panic in Mrs. S.'s eyes. "Are you going?" "Yes, I have to cook for my boys." "Don't leave me." What was this? She had just told me how I was no help at all, and what was I doing there. Now she did not want me to go, even though she also did not want me there. "Twenty minutes," I agreed, reluctantly.

Those twenty minutes extended several times. She got me to agree to stay until dinner time. There was another trip to the bathroom. As the nurse came to take her, she said to me venomously, "You will probably leave while I am gone." "No," I said, "I promised you that I would stay with you until dinner is served, so that is what I will do. I am making my own boys wait for their dinner, in order to be with you."

When Mrs. S. returned from the bathroom, I was waiting for her. She took my hand and held it, possessively. Then finally dinner was served. I loosened her grip on my hand, stood up and said that I was going. I had kept my promise. She was anything but grateful. Looking at me with accusing eyes, she shot at me, "And who will be here with me until I go to bed?" "Mrs. S., I do not know, but I have to take care of my boys now." I took Pippa's leash, entered the code that limits access to the elevator, and disappeared.

Looking at the story as the story, without making it prettier than it is, is essential to seeing God's story in the one before you. Not all encounters on the ward are as stark as this one was, but this one seemed important to include. This question mark in the dark is also *hineni*, and it feels like singing into a darkened concert hall, with no applause at the end.

Chapter Conclusions

The contributors have shown us that *hineni* is not merely a professional attitude to be employed in a session, but a way of being in and relating to the world that expresses itself also in the practice of spiritual direction. For some, it is a way of life. They have also shown that *hineni* as it applies to spiritual direction seems to have three elements: preparation for, receptivity and awareness during, and reaction to the mystery of the other, to the God in the other, from the God in the director.

These examples are not meant to be templates. They give glimpses of how several spiritual directors try to live *hineni*, in their unique ways, in imitation of Abraham. The God of Abraham, the God of Isaac, and the God of Jacob is also the God of Awraham, the God of Leo, the God of Blanche, the God of Peter, the God of Jana, the God of Hein, the God of Pippa, and the God of Alisa. Their stories invite us to make the Name, too. Embodied *hineni* is what we seek to imitate, each in our own inimitable way.

Each directee comes dressed in a narrative. It is not our job to resolve or make sense of it. Each story is fundamentally vulnerable and must be allowed to remain that way. The experience is the experience, as it is, in the moment. We do not need to make it holy, but to see the holiness in it, to let the holiness in it reveal itself. This means coming empty, open, and vulnerable ourselves, and letting the word of God before us speak his or her truth, say his or her own *hineni*. It means letting ourselves be blessed, even as we hope to be a blessing to others. It means daring to be present to what is, to listen for God's story in it, with the ear of the heart.

Journeying with others cannot help but give shape to a spiritual director's own journey. A spiritual director needs to pursue God in his or her own depth in order to recognize that pursuit in another. Accompanying has everything to do with our own lived spiritual lives. The other inevitably acts as a mirror for us. So being there for others asks us to be there for ourselves, attending to our spiritual lives in meaningful and embodied ways. It asks us to be aware of what we are bringing and to see the beautiful one-sidedness of it as well.

There are a few commonalities in these unique stories:

- The mystics are a touchstone.

- Practices develop intention and desire for *hineni.*

- There is a deep respect for the mystery of the other.

- Boundaries, even paradoxical ones, guard holiness.

- Verbs of action include seek, hope, and focus.

- *Hineni* remains *yes* in the moment, to what the moment asks—it is a constantly renewed assent. *Hineni* is, despite—and even because of—the director's limitations. It is not dependent on experience or expertise but beyond them.

Hineni can shake the sense of security of both directee and director. Equally, it can feel spacious and liberating. *Hineni* means being open to the inspiration of the Spirit of God and to the working of grace. It can be transformational and greater than the sum of the parts. Some directors seek to awaken the master in the one before them, while others note the possibility that the moment will ask them to wait or be open to surprise. Awareness and focus/concentration need to be simultaneous. All affirm that *hineni* involves open expectancy and is an inner orientation with expression in external responses. Some would call that incarnation. *Hineni* is making the Name, being *Here I Am* to the one before us.

Each respondent holds the tensions of mystery and oneness, awareness and embodiment, connection and commitment, openness to receive, directional and in the moment. Each of them stands in a different place and moves in different ways, between each of the complementary or paradoxical pairs, but each does hold, rather than resolve them. How fortunate to have their living wisdom add to the long and rich tradition of spiritual direction.

Since the completion of this book, both Pippa and Leo have died. Each of them was a larger-than-life presence for those of us who knew and loved them. May the lessons they taught with their lives live on in our hearts, and may their memories be for a blessing.

IV

Conclusion

How do we meet the mystery of the other? How does *hineni*, in imitation of Abraham, help a spiritual director respond to the mystery? Here is where it gets tricky and words like ineffable become appropriate. Seeking the mystery in the other is really seeking the mystery in me. The light reflected in the shard of the other mirrors the light in the self.

This book is as personal to me as the story of Abraham was to him. Writing it has been its own journey, a way of seeking my gate of entrance into the mystery that I love.

The name of my gate is *hineni*. Writing this book has caused me to knock on and push and kick the gate. I have examined how others, on their way, approach the gate called *hineni*. Studying the gate has been a way of opening it, maybe even a way of realizing what, in the depth of me, I knew all along but still had to figure out for myself. Entering into the mystery through the gate that opens for me, while it does not give access to the mystery, not really, cannot help but be transformative, because love, work, and desire make and reveal hidden oneness. This is the most honest response.

However, there is more to it.

I started with an analysis of the paradigmatic story of Abraham and Isaac—this is the particular. From that analysis, certain universals emerged. *Hineni* is directional. It means letting go of who we thought or think we were in order to become more and more who we are in our depths. *Hineni* is not merely an intellectual assent, but lived and embodied. *Hineni* is a response from a fundamental oneness that we can recognize, even in a stranger, if we listen with the ear of the heart. It is yes to a mystery we can barely begin to fathom.

I then looked at what these conclusions might mean for a spiritual direction practice, first acknowledging the warning that we have no idea what we have said *hineni* to and we have no idea what we will encounter. Proceeding then means real trust.

In spiritual direction, *hineni* means being open to interruption, while maintaining boundaries. It means admitting that, in a way, we are inadequate to the task, and that skill might be less important than the humanity of the whole self, which also includes incapacity. It means willingness and openness both to give and receive, as well as letting go of the hierarchical desire to fix. Fixing and solving do not work, because they deny the oneness hidden in the impenetrable mystery. Not only do we have no idea what we will encounter, but, as Hein noted, God is not a problem to be solved. Putting in our whole selves means trusting even when, perhaps especially when, every instinct cries out to grab the controls of self-preservation. Spiritual direction means being that vulnerable, as well as being vigilant, acknowledging mystery and oneness, and being in the now while having a direction. Spiritual direction is not for the faint-hearted.

These conclusions were tested, though not in a scientific way, by soliciting the experiences of seasoned spiritual directors in order to determine if and how their lived practice supports my initial conclusions. The respondents indeed confirm and enhance the conclusions through the lenses of their own rich experiences. They show us that *hineni* is a disposition, a way of being in the world and that we can learn a lot from the mystics, who left descriptions of their unique ways. Lifting the shard of another can help to awaken the master, the one who is ready to walk on his own, in the directee. They show that the surprise, the coincidence of the moment, just might be divine, and that putting in our whole selves will change us in ways that cannot be imagined.

This is why seeking God in all things is a disposition, as constantly renewed assent is a disposition. *Hineni* requires listening and the direction relationship is irrevocably reciprocal. A director holds paradoxes, rather than forcing resolution. Therefore, we can conclude that *hineni* truly is fundamental and unmissable in the practice of spiritual direction.

In the end, there is only one mystery, and the mystery includes everything and everyone. Whether an individual touches that infinite mystery in him- or herself, in another, or through a mythical story or music or dogs does not matter. This is an important awareness for any spiritual director. A directee does not have to talk about God to be talking about God.

Maybe *hineni* is simply being a *Mensch*: seeing, being moved to one's depths with compassion and, from there, acting; being open and willing, putting one's whole self in and allowing space for the other, so that the surprise inherent in the moment can occur. Maybe allowing the space to bless and be blessed is *tzimtzum*, too.

We do not know who or what God is. One filling in of the name, and the empty spaces between the letters of YHWH says that it is a present-tense verb meaning what is happening now. The mystics, both Jewish and Christian, tell us that God does not have beingness. This implies that, for "God to happen" on this earth, God needs to happen through creation and through us. Saying *hineni* is assent to God happening in the one who assents, to that covenant, that partnership. It is Mary's "yes."

You, dear reader, are a mystery. I do not know how God works in you. All I know is that these words are here for you, like seeds sown. The harvest is not for me. In that sense, the book becomes autonomous. Each person who reads it will develop his or her own relationship with it, as I did with Genesis 22.

My work with people living with dementia reveals the truth of Thomas Merton's untouched, untouchable point in the self.[1] Hein wrote, "There is no real difference between the person who tells a 'rational story' and the person who speaks in a very enigmatic or even strange way. In both cases, I will have to listen to the person 'behind' the obviously present person." People living with dementia demonstrate both the otherness of the other and the hidden oneness.

Relationships with those living with dementia are revealing in other ways, as well. There is not much room for hidden agendas, and so it is clearer to me when I come with one. That stripped-down reality makes me wonder whose reality is more real. Those with dementia are developing subjects, too. They are *becoming*. How can I best companion people with whom connection through language is not always possible, so that they can sense meaning and maintain dignity and integrity? I constantly wonder if dementia, if such a radical stripping down, means, paradoxically, that the person is becoming more who he is in his depth.

As for the question, "how do we meet the mystery of the other," we don't, not really. We acknowledge it, respect it, stand in awe of it, while, at the same time, suspecting it contains a hidden oneness. In this sense, being a spiritual director is learning to walk in the dark, in a perpetual question mark.

And yet, Jana's husband, Charlie, who is a priest and poet, reminds me that "When two meet, really meet, and are present, God is [in] the presence." He wonders—and I with him—if a deeper communion occurs when two people are *hineni* for each other. Maybe that is the beyond, that space in which the *I* and the *you* again sink, for a moment, into oneness.

This book is an embodied version of *hineni* itself, a way of living the business of the words. It has been working, seeking, and desiring, toward oneness with or in that presence. The space of *hineni* is still inviting me to be and to become. *Sit finis libri, non finis quaerendi*—the book is finished, but the seeking goes on.

Notes

Introduction

1. Lawrence Troster, "Here I Am: Responding to the Call in Creation" (November 20, 2011), http://jewcology.org/2011/11/here-i-am -responding-to-the-call-in-creation/.

2. Adele Berlin and Marc Zvi, eds., *The Jewish Study Bible* (New York: Oxford University Press, 2004), 45.

3. Marc de Kesel, Lecture 5, May 31, 2017.

4. Leo de Jong, "God as Direction of Our Seeking" (January 2014), http://www.hetsteiger.nl/images/stories/documenten/boeken_Leo _de_Jong/God%20als%20zoekrichting.pdf, 5.

5. Muriel Rukeyser, *The Gates* (New York: McGraw-Hill, 1976), 17.

6. Lawrence Kushner, "Kabbalah and the Inner Life of God," interview by Krista Tippett, *On Being*, NPR, March 10, 2016, transcript, https://onbeing.org/programs/lawrence-kushner-kabbalah-and-the-inner -life-of-god/.

7. Rachel Naomi Remen, "Kabbalah and the Inner Life of God," interview by Krista Tippett, *On Being*, NPR, March 10, 2016, transcript, https://onbeing.org/programs/lawrence-kushner-kabbalah-and-the-inner-life-of-god/.

8. David M. Goodman and Scott F. Grover, "Hineni and Transference: The Remembering and Forgetting of the Other," *Pastoral Psychology* 56, no. 6 (July 2008): 562.

9. Gerald May, *Will and Spirit: A Contemplative Psychology* (New York: HarperCollins, 1987), 6.

10. Caryll Houselander, *The Reed of God* (Notre Dame: Ave Maria Press, 2006), 21.

I Genesis 22—A *Midrash*

1. Yehuda Sherpin, *Why No Vowels in the Torah?*, https://www.chabad.org/library/article_cdo/aid/3087993/jewish/Why-No-Vowels-in-the-Torah.htm.

2. Jena Schwartz, "The Space Between the Consonants," On Being Blog, January 16, 2016, https://onbeing.org/blog/the-spaces-between-the-consonants.

3. Gershom Scholem, *On the Kabbalah and Its Symbolism* (New York: Random House, 1996), 29–31. (From "Kabbalah and the Inner Life of God," interview by Krista Tippett, *On Being*, NPR, March 10, 2016.)

4. Rav Alex Israel, "Abraham's Journey," http://etzion.org.il/en/abrahams-journey.

5. Cited in Elie Wiesel, "The Sacrifice of Isaac: A Survivor's Story," in *Messengers of God: Biblical Portraits and Legends* (New York: Random House, 1976), 72.

6. Jos Huls, *Being Seen in God: (Human Hiddenness and) Kierkegaard's Call to Gaze in the Mirror of the Word*, Studies in Spirituality Supplement 29 (Leuven: Peeters Publishers, 2017).

7. The translation used is the NRSV, with Lord and God changed to YHWH and Elohim, respectively, as per Harris Lenowitz, "The Binding of Isaac: A View of Jewish Exegesis," *Dialogue: A Journal of Mormon Thought*, 92–93, https://www.dialoguejournal.com/wp-content/uploads/sbi/articles/Dialogue_V20N02_92.pdf.

8. Sharon Sobel, "Hineni: Here I Am," New York, September 25, 2014, http://www.rabbisharonsobel.com/sermons/rh-day-2014/.

9. Medinah Korn, "And He Answered, Here I Am: An Educational Model for the Rabbi Solveitchik's Halakhah of Suffering" (Jerusalem: Academy for Torah Initiatives and Directives, 2005), 4–5.

10. Goodman and Grover, "Hineni and Transference," 563.

11. John I. Lawlor, "The Test of Abraham: Genesis 22:1-19," *Grace Theological Journal*, 19. See https://biblicalstudies.org.uk/pdf/gtj/01-1_019.pdf.

12. For example, Rashi writes out an argument, Wiesel believes he should have argued.

13. Lawlor, "The Test of Abraham," 19.

14. Lawlor, 19.

15. Wiesel, "The Sacrifice of Isaac," 81–82.

16. Lawlor, 22.

17. As stated by Hein Blommestijn in lectures.

18. Jonathan Sacks, "To Bless the Space Between Us" (October 26, 2015), http://rabbisacks.org/to-bless-the-space-between-us-vayera-5776/.

19. Sacks, "To Bless the Space Between Us."

20. Marc de Kesel, Lecture 5, May 31, 2017.

21. Steven Shankman, "Rembrandt's *The Sacrifice of Isaac*, Abraham's Suspended Knife, and the Face of the Other" (SUNY Press), 4, http://www.sunypress.edu/pdf/61866.pdf.

22. Shankman, "Rembrandt's *The Sacrifice of Isaac*," 7.

23. Richard McBee, "Rembrandt's Abraham Etchings at Swann Galleries" (May 6, 2008), http://richardmcbee.com/writings/museums/item/rembrandt-s-abraham.

24. Ellen F. Davis, *Getting Involved with God: Rediscovering the Old Testament* (Plymouth, UK: Rowman and Littlefield, 2001), 58.

25. Wiesel, "The Sacrifice of Isaac," 72–73.

26. Norman J. Cohen, *Hineini in Our Lives* (Nashville: Jewish Lights Publishing, 2003), 23.

27. Wiesel, "The Sacrifice of Isaac," 90.

28. Korn, "And He Answered, Here I Am," 6.

29. Walter Brueggemann, *Genesis: A Bible Commentary for Teaching and Preaching* (Atlanta: John Knox Press, 1982), 185.

30. Kushner, "Kabbalah and the Inner Life of God."

31. Sacks, "To Bless the Space Between Us."

32. Brian Pizzalato, "Covenant, Sacraments Divinely Linked," https://www.catholicnewsagency.com/resources/sacraments/sacraments/covenant-sacraments-divinely-linked.

33. Jos Huls, *Faith in the Face of Death: Interpretation of Kierkegaard's Meditations on Abraham's Sacrifice*, Studies in Spirituality Supplement 21 (Leuven: Peeters Publishers, 2011), 331.

34. Korn, "And He Answered, Here I Am," 5.

35. Edmund Colledge, OSA, and Bernard McGinn, *Meister Eckhart, The Essential Sermons, Commentaries, Treatises and Defense* (Mahwah, NJ: Paulist Press, 1981), 200.

36. Wiesel, "The Sacrifice of Isaac," 83.

37. Ari Kaiman, "Searching the Meaning of 'Hineni—I am Here,'" *STL Jewish Light*, January 4, 2012, http://www.stljewishlight.com/opinion/dvar_torah/article_802594b2-3708-11e1-b672-001871e3ce6c.html.

38. Charles Merrill, "Carl Rogers and Martin Buber in Dialogue: The Meeting of Divergent Paths," *The Person-Centered Journal* 15, no.

1–2 (2008): 3, http://www.adpca.org/system/files/documents/journal/Merrill-Carl_Rogers_and_Martin_Buber_in_Dialogue-PCJ_15_1-2_2008.pdf.

39. Korn, "And He Answered, Here I Am," 5.

40. Korn, 4–5.

41. Huls, *Faith in the Face of Death*, 312.

42. Israel, "Abraham's Journey."

43. Brueggemann, *Genesis*, 192–93.

44. William Stafford, *The Way It Is* (Minneapolis: Graywolf Press, 1998), 247.

II *Hineni*: Making the Name and the Practice of Spiritual Direction

1. Steven Paulikas, "How Should We Respond to Evil?," *The New York Times*, June 27, 2016, https://www.nytimes.com/2016/06/27/opinion/how-should-we-respond-to-evil.html.

2. Brueggemann, *Genesis*, 188–91.

3. Stafford, *The Way It Is*, 247.

4. De Kesel, Lecture 5.

5. Henri Nouwen, *Out of Solitude* (Notre Dame: Ave Maria Press, 1974), 56.

6. From the prayer "Christ Has No Body Now But Yours," attributed to St. Teresa of Avila.

7. Cohen, *Hineini in Our Lives*, 13.

8. Cohen, 11.

9. Etty Hillesum, *An Interrupted Life* (New York: Holt and Co., 1996), 44.

10. Huls, *Faith in the Face of Death*, 335.

11. Cohen, *Hineini in Our Lives*, 127.

12. Cohen, 127.

13. Richard Rohr, "Absolute Vulnerability," from *Daily Meditations*, Wednesday, March 8, 2017.

14. Cohen, *Hineini in Our Lives*, 126.

15. Martin Buber, *Two Types of Faith* (New York: Macmillan, 1986), 7.

16. Huls, *Faith in the Face of Death*, 332.

17. Cohen, *Hineini in our Lives*, 158.

18. De Jong, "God as Direction of Our Seeking," 9.

19. Cohen, *Hineini in Our Lives*, 138.

20. Cohen, 136.

III Collected Wisdom from the Field

1. Patricia Burlin Kennedy and Robert Christie, *Through Otis' Eyes: Lessons from a Guide Dog Puppy* (New York: Howell Book House, 1998).

IV Conclusion

1. Thomas Merton, *Conjectures of a Guilty Bystander* (New York: Doubleday, 1966), 140–42.

Bibliography

Astor, Yaakov. *Me, Myself and I: Ethics of the Fathers.* http://www
.aish.com/sp/pg/48893292.html.

Barry, William A., and William J. Connolly. *The Practice of Spiritual Direction.* New York: HarperCollins, 1982.

Bergant, Diane, and Robert J. Karris, eds. *The Collegeville Bible Commentary.* Collegeville, MN: Liturgical Press, 1988.

Berlin, Adele, and Marc Zvi Brettler, eds. *The Jewish Study Bible.* New York: Oxford University Press, 2004.

Bregman, Marc. "Midrash as Visualization." *Journal of Textual Reasoning.* http://jtr.shanti.virginia.edu/volume-2-number-1 /aqedah-midrash-as-visualization/.

Brown, Brené. *Daring Greatly.* New York: Penguin Random House, 2012.

Brown, Raymond Edward, ed. *The Jerome Biblical Commentary.* Englewood Cliffs, NJ: Prentice-Hall, 1968.

Brueggemann, Walter. *Genesis: A Bible Commentary for Teaching and Preaching.* Atlanta: John Knox Press, 1982.

Buber, Martin. *I and Thou.* New York: Scribner, 1987.

———. *Two Types of Faith.* New York: Macmillan, 1986.

Cohen, Norman J. *Hineini in Our Lives.* Nashville: Jewish Lights Publishing, 2003.

Colledge, Edmund, OSA, and Bernard McGinn. *Meister Eckhart, The Essential Sermons, Commentaries, Treatises and Defense.* Mahwah, NJ: Paulist Press, 1981.

Coogan, Michael D. et al. *Oxford Biblical Studies Online.* Oxford University Press. http://www.oxfordbiblicalstudies.com/.

Davis, Ellen F. *Getting Involved with God: Rediscovering the Old Testament.* Plymouth, UK: Rowman and Littlefield, 2001.

Derrida, Jacques. *Abraham, the Other.* In *Judeities: Questions for Jacques Derrida.* Translated by Bettina Bergo and Michael B. Smith. New York: Fordham University Press, 2007. http://users.clas.ufl.edu/burt/KafkaKierkegaardBible/derrida otherabrahamjudeities.pdf.

Edelglass, William. "Levinas in Suffering and Compassion." *Sophia* 45, no. 2 (October 2006). https://www.academia.edu/7128672/Levinas_on_Suffering_and_Compassion_2006.

Frankl, Viktor E. *Man's Search for Meaning.* Boston: Beacon Press, 2006.

Goodman, David M., and Scott F. Grover. "Hineni and Transference: The Remembering and Forgetting of the Other." *Pastoral Psychology* 56, no. 6 (July 2008): 561–71.

Houselander, Caryll. *The Reed of God.* Notre Dame: Ave Maria Press, 2006.

Huls, Jos. *Being Seen in God: (Human Hiddenness and) Kierkegaard's Call to Gaze in the Mirror of the Word.* Studies in Spirituality Supplements 29. Leuven: Peeters Publishers, 2017.

————. *Faith in the Face of Death: Interpretation of Kierkegaard's Meditations on Abraham's Sacrifice.* Studies in Spirituality Supplement 21. Leuven: Peeters Publishers, 2011.

Israel, Rav Alex. "Abraham's Journey." http://etzion.org.il/en /abrahams-journey.

de Jong, Leo. "God as Direction of Our Seeking." January 2014. http:// www.hetsteiger.nl/images/stories/documenten/boeken _Leo_de_Jong/God%20als%20zoekrichting.pdf.

Kafka, Franz. *Abraham.* http://zork.net/~patty/pattyland/kafka /parables/abraham.htm.

Kaiman, Ari. "Searching the Meaning of 'Hineni—I am Here.'" *STL Jewish Light.* January 4, 2012. http://www.stljewish light.com/opinion/dvar_torah/article_802594b2-3708 -11e1-b672-001871e3ce6c.html.

Katz, Amy Wallk. "Here I Am: Hineni." http://www.tbespringfield .org/here-i-am-hineni.

Katz, Claire Elise. "The Voice of God and the Face of the Other: Levinas, Kierkegaard, and Abraham." Penn State University, 2001. http://www.sorenkierkegaard.nl/artikelen/Engels /043.%20The%20Voice%20of%20God%20and%20the%20 Face%20of%20the%20Other.pdf.

Keating, Stephen. "Presentation on Derrida's The Gift of Death." https://itself.blog/2014/02/19/presentation-on-derridas -the-gift-of-death/.

Kierkegaard, Søren. *Fear and Trembling.* Princeton: Princeton University Press, 1983.

Korn, Medinah. "And He Answered, Here I Am: An Educational Model for the Rabbi Solveitchik's Halakhah of Suffering." Jerusalem: Academy for Torah Initiatives and Directives, 2005.

Kushner, Lawrence. "Kabbalah and the Inner Life of God." Interview by Krista Tippett, *On Being.* NPR, March 10, 2016 (transcript). https://onbeing.org/programs/lawrence-kushner-kabbalah-and-the-inner-life-of-god/.

Lawlor, John I. "The Test of Abraham: Genesis 22:1-19." *Grace Theological Journal.* https://biblicalstudies.org.uk/pdf/gtj/01-1_019.pdf.

Lenowitz, Harris. "The Binding of Isaac: A View of Jewish Exegesis." *Dialogue: A Journal of Mormon Thought*, 92–93. https://www.dialoguejournal.com/wp-content/uploads/sbi/articles/Dialogue_V20N02_92.pdf.

Levinas, Emanuel. "A Propos of 'Kierkegaard Vivant.'" In *Proper Names*, translated by Michael B. Smith, 75–79. Stanford: Stanford University Press, 1996.

Marseille, Jeremias. "The Spiritual Dimension in Logotherapy: Viktor Frankl's Contribution to Transpersonal Psychology." *The Journal of Transpersonal Psychology* 29, no. 11 (1997).

May, Gerald. *The Awakened Heart: Opening Yourself to the Love You Need.* New York: HarperCollins, 1991.

———. *Care of Mind, Care of Spirit.* New York: HarperCollins, 1992.

———. *The Dark Night of the Soul: A Psychiatrist Explores the Connection Between Darkness and Spiritual Growth.* New York: HarperCollins, 2004.

———. *Will and Spirit: A Contemplative Psychology.* New York: HarperCollins, 1987.

McBee, Richard. "Rembrandt's Abraham Etchings at Swann Galleries." May 6, 2008. http://richardmcbee.com/writings/museums/item/rembrandt-s-abraham.

Merrill, Charles. "Carl Rogers and Martin Buber in Dialogue: The Meeting of Divergent Paths." *The Person-Centered Journal* 15, no. 1–2 (2008). http://www.adpca.org/system/files/documents/journal/Merrill-Carl_Rogers_and_Martin_Buber_in_Dialogue-PCJ_15_1-2_2008.pdf.

Merton, Thomas. *Spiritual Direction and Meditation.* Collegeville, MN: Liturgical Press, 1960.

Nouwen, Henri J. M. *Out of Solitude.* Notre Dame: Ave Maria Press, 1974.

———. *Spiritual Direction.* New York: HarperCollins, 2006.

———. *Spiritual Formation: Following the Movements of the Spirit.* New York: HarperCollins, 2010.

———. *The Wounded Healer: Ministry in Contemporary Society.* New York: Doubleday, 2010.

O'Donohue, John. *To Bless the Space Between Us.* New York: Doubleday, 2008.

Paulikas, Steven. "How Should We Respond to Evil?" *The New York Times*, June 27, 2016. https://www.nytimes.com/2016/06/27/opinion/how-should-we-respond-to-evil.html.

Pizzalato, Brian. "Covenant, Sacraments Divinely Linked." https://www.catholicnewsagency.com/resources/sacraments/sacraments/covenant-sacraments-divinely-linked.

Rohr, Richard. *Loving Fully.* Daily Meditation, Wednesday, December 13, 2017.

Rosenbaum, M., and A. M. Silbermann. *Rashi Chumash (Rashi's Commentary on Genesis).* Metsudah Publications, 2009. https://www.sefaria.org/Rashi_on_Genesis.22.1.1?vhe=Wikitext&lang=bi&with=About&lang2=en.

Sacks, Jonathan. "To Bless the Space Between Us." October 26, 2015. http://rabbisacks.org/to-bless-the-space-between-us-vayera-5776/.

———. "Covenant and Conversation—The Binding of Isaac: A New Interpretation." Orthodox Union, October 23, 2010. https://www.ou.org/torah/parsha/rabbi-sacks-on-parsha/the_binding_of_isaac_a_new_interpretation/.

———. "The Binding of Isaac." November 3, 2014. http://rabbisacks.org/binding-isaac-vayera-5775/.

Scholem, Gershom. *On the Kabbalah and Its Symbolism.* New York: Random House, 1996.

Schwartz, Jena. "The Space Between the Consonants." On Being Blog, January 16, 2016. https://onbeing.org/blog/the-spaces-between-the-consonants/.

Scott, John G. et al. "Healing Relationships and the Existential Philosophy of Martin Buber." *Journal of Philosophy, Ethics and Humanities in Medicine* 4 (2009). http://www.ncbi.nlm.nih.gov/pmc/articles/PMC2733137/.

Shankman, Steven. "Rembrandt's *The Sacrifice of Isaac*, Abraham's Suspended Knife, and the Face of the Other." http://www.sunypress.edu/pdf/61866.pdf.

Shurpin, Yehuda. "Why No Vowels in the Torah?" https://www.chabad.org/library/article_cdo/aid/3087993/jewish/Why-No-Vowels-in-the-Torah.htm.

Signer, Michael A. "Rashi's Reading of the Akedah." *Journal of Textual Reasoning.* http://jtr.shanti.virginia.edu/volume-2-number-1/rashis-reading-of-the-akedah/.

Sobel, Sharon. "Hineni: Here I Am." New York, September 25, 2014. http://www.rabbisharonsobel.com/sermons/rh-day-2014/.

Steindl-Rast, David. *The Way of Silence: Engaging the Sacred in Daily Life.* Cincinnati: Franciscan Media, 2016.

Troster, Lawrence. "Here I Am: Responding to the Call in Creation." November 20, 2011. http://jewcology.org/2011/11/here-i-am -responding-to-the-call-in-creation/.

Wiesel, Elie. "The Sacrifice of Isaac: A Survivor's Story." In *Messengers of God: Biblical Portraits and Legends.* New York: Random House, 1976.

Vanier, Jean. *Encountering 'the Other.'* Mahwah, NJ: Paulist Press, 2006.